Craft: An Argument

*Why the term 'Craft Beer' is completely undefinable,
hopelessly misunderstood and absolutely essential*

Pete Brown

STORM LANTERN
PUBLICATIONS

CRAFT: AN ARGUMENT
Why craft beer is completely undefinable, hopelessly
misunderstood, and absolutely essential

Published by Storm Lantern Publications
52 Bayston Road
London
N16 7LT

First Published June 2020

ISBN 978-1-8380498-1-2

Praise for
"Craft: An Argument"

"One of the leading beer thinkers of our time, Pete delivers up well crafted, important insights into the nature of modern brewing. A must-read for brewers wanting to find their sense of place amongst the shifting sands of marketing, business, consumers and trends."

Matt Kirkegaard, Brews News, Australia

"In 2009's Hops and Glory, Pete Brown took a cask to India in order to reveal the true nature of India pale ale. In 2020's Craft: An Argument, he does the metaphorical equivalent to arrive at the meaning of 'craft' as it pertains to beer. While the journey is certainly shorter, it is no less rigorous, compelling, or splendidly entertaining."

Stephen Beaumont, co-author, "The World Atlas of Beer", Canada

"Exciting and exuberant, this is a fascinating and fantastically articulate argument and polemic that heads straight to the heart of craft beer, written by a master craftsman at the height of his literary powers."

Adrian Tierney-Jones, "1001 Beers You Must Try Before You Die", UK

3

To Liz,
Who did every single thing
to bring this book to life
apart from writing it.

Contents

#SELLOUT

Thursday 21ˢᵗ May 2018 dawns sunny and warm, after a typically fitful few days when the English weather kind of knew it was meant to be drifting into high summer but couldn't really be bothered. It's finally made up its mind. With any luck, the covers will be coming off the nation's barbecues this weekend.

This change in the weather makes the bubble community that refers to itself as #BeerTwitter seem all the darker. Because here, unlike outside, storm clouds have been gathering for weeks. If Twitter had virtual dogs they would be fractious and bad-tempered. If the bird in the famous logo could sing, it would have stopped.

At 9.36am, the storm finally breaks.

It starts with North London craft brewery Beavertown posting a tweet, that in turn links to a press release containing the most significant announcement in the company's seven-year history.

The team looking after the brewery's social media account have just begun possibly the busiest and most stressful day of their professional lives.

The reaction is immediate.

"Absolutely pathetic, simple greed, no loyalty to customer base. I loved your beers [but] that's me and sadly many more finished with Beavertown #greed #sellout."

"Absolutely gutted. Why do you guys feel you have to take over the world? I've been a fan for so long I'm so disappointed."

"Just opened Pandora'$ box my friends. It's like Anakin Skywalker getting a taste of the Dark side."

And most often, and most poignantly,

"Bye then."

By lunchtime, independent craft beer shop Hop Burns & Black – for whom Beavertown's beers make up eight per cent of their total sales – has made a public announcement that it will no longer be stocking Beavertown beers. The language of the open letter to the brewery makes it clear that this was a decision full of anguish, borne not of business logic but of genuinely felt emotional pain, perhaps even grief.

Next, Cloudwater – possibly the coolest name in craft beer in June 2018 – announces that it is pulling out of the Beavertown Extravaganza, an event planned for November that sounded like it was going to be craft beer's answer to the Glastonbury Festival, with the best craft brewers from around the world onsite representing their beers. Around half the breweries who have signed up for the event will soon follow Cloudwater out of the door.

The comments keep coming. Most of those addressed directly back to the brewery are polite, and there are many wishing the brewery well and congratulating them. But as "hot takes" start appearing across beer blogs and the twitter feeds of podcasters, so too does the use of those hashtags, #sellout and #greed.

At 4.30pm, BrewDog – the giant of the UK craft beer scene – announces that it too is withdrawing from the Beavertown Extravaganza – and also withdrawing Beavertown's beers from sale across its nationwide chain of bars.
It feels like a disastrous day. What kind of scandal could Beavertown have announced to create such genuine rage and heartbreak, to see its closest peers distance themselves from the brewery so quickly?

Simple: after denying that they ever would, Beavertown has just committed craft beer's cardinal sin: in order to fund the next phase of their rapid expansion, Beavertown has sold a stake in the business to corporate giant Heineken.

"Funny how Logan praises the quality of their brewing when last year he called [out] their beers as crap fizzy yellow shite!!"

"Heineken are The enemies of Independent brewing. This shit

10

[Beavertown founder Logan Plant] is talking is from the same script everyone is given when they Sell. Good luck! But don't piss on our backs and tell us its raining."

"Once the big guys have [brands like] these, they're no more authentically craft than the brands that bought them."

To some, this reaction feels a little over the top: Beavertown is a business that wants to expand. Is that a crime? It's not as if Heineken has taken overall control of the company – the deal is for a minority stake, the exact amount of which is not disclosed (but is in all likelihood 49%) and Logan Plant and his family still retain overall control of the business.

Also, it's not as if Beavertown is the first craft brewery to do this. In the United States, Goose Island was acquired outright by Anheuser-Busch InBev in 2011. Heineken bought half of Lagunitas in 2015, and took the other half in 2017. Even here in London, we should be used to this by now: In 2015, SABMiller bought Meantime and AB InBev bought Camden Town. There wasn't half as much outcry six months ago, when Heineken made their first foray into London craft brewing by buying 49% of the Brixton Brewery.

But none of those was Beavertown. This is like that time when you got caught cheating by your favourite teacher: "I expected this kind of mischief from your stupid friend, but not you – I always thought you were a model pupil."

Meantime? Whatever. But Beavertown? This is Dylan going electric. Geri leaving the Spice Girls. The Brooklyn Dodgers moving to LA. Combined.

This is not about business. This is about remaining faithful to an ideal. This is about morality…

Preface

This book began life as an exercise in pedantry, and an attempt to wind you up.

I had become bored and frustrated – as many beer devotees have – of the endless debate in beer circles over the meaning of the term "craft beer", and yet I couldn't leave it alone. I kept returning to it, picking at it like a scab on a wound you know would heal quicker if you left it alone. I'd weigh in every time I saw a discussion arise on social media. I wrote blog posts and gave presentations at conferences about it that came from a contrarian position to whatever the prevailing mood was around the term at that time. I shifted my own stance and contradicted myself, if I had to, in order to counter any point I found annoying.

Each attempt at an "official" definition from an industry body would only intensify the argument, with people attacking it for being too simplistic or too self-serving, for making craft beer too niche or for making it too mainstream. The only thing that made people angrier than attempts to define craft beer in clear, measurable terms was other people saying maybe it didn't need to be defined in clear, measurable terms. And so, round and round it went, year after year.

Meanwhile, craft beer just got bigger and bigger, until even people who had no interest in defining craft beer and no awareness of the furious debate around doing so were enthusiastically drinking it. This incensed some of the people who were *really* into craft beer, who argued that we now needed a definition more urgently than ever, to protect the virtue of craft beer as it grew big enough to attract admiring glances from the brewers and drinkers of generic, mass-market industrial lagers, and enraged others still more who felt that if craft beer was getting this big then it wasn't

13

craft beer any more – its commercial success proving beyond doubt that it didn't actually exist at all as a meaningful concept that had anything to do with ideas of craft.

Many of my friends and colleagues in the beer world grew tired of this perpetual quarrel, or realised it was getting in the way of them enjoying great beer, and just let it drop, or ended up taking positions such as "You know it when you see it (or taste it)" or "Good beer is just good beer." Needless to say, such opinions made other people apoplectic all over again.

I enjoy probing such intractable puzzles the way people whose brains are wired up differently from mine enjoy cryptic crossword puzzles. But I was getting nowhere close to solving this one. It's a debate that sometimes becomes ridiculous. So eventually, I decided to get ridiculous about it.

I enjoy public speaking. The anxiety I feel if I'm asked to work a room, to circulate and mingle, disappears if I'm asked instead to go out on a stage and address that room while shielded by a lectern or microphone. I'm often invited to speak at both public-facing and beer industry events. If I'm not given a specific topic to speak on, I have a small collection of off-the-shelf talks I can wheel out. The ones I had were getting well-worn, so I decided to write a short, humorous talk on the meaning of craft beer for a pub and bar trade show I was speaking at in February 2019. In a playful fashion, I wanted to intellectualise the debate around the meaning of craft beer to a ridiculous degree, to make it unbearably pretentious. After seeing the word in a book that said quite a lot about craft but not about beer, I said we should forget craft beer and go back to its original spelling, and talk about *cræft* beer instead. Given the underlying nature of the craft beer debate, I expected to annoy people, but hoped I'd get some enjoyment out of doing so.

It didn't go as planned.

14

My small audience really enjoyed the talk. They laughed, but they also engaged with the points I was making. They started tweeting about *craft* beer.

I fleshed out the talk and repeated it at other events, pushed its absurd reach even further. I incorporated post-structuralism and semiotics. Surely my audiences wouldn't sit through this with a straight face? Obviously, they'd either get angry with me or just laugh and walk away, making crude hand gestures as they did so?

They did neither. They applauded – one woman even cried – and urged me to apply to other, bigger conferences and festivals to repeat the talk there. Then they asked when the book was coming out. What book? Why does everyone think that if I talk about something I must be writing a book about it? I'm not that predicable surely? There was no book. There wasn't going to be a book. They told me there had to be, that I had to write it.

Still feeling playful, I decided to write a short tract – an essay – that I still suspected (and partially hoped) people would read to the end and then throw across the room in frustration.

That was enough to get me doing the kind of reading and research I do when I *am* writing a book. And just like it always does, that research sucked me in way deeper than I had planned. Each thing I read led me to more things to read, until I was devouring book after book that didn't mention beer at all, but talked about a broader conception of the idea of "craft" that incorporated topics as varied as woodworking, shoemaking, organisational theory and behaviour, Cartesian duality and linguistics. The more I read, the more a serious argument formed that felt too important to throw away by taking the piss. I dropped the snark – or at least most of it. Some of these books made me think about my life, and how I spend it, in entirely new ways. As I learned why "craft" matters, I realised that the debate over craft beer had lost the point, and become a discussion that wasn't really about "craft" at all. As beer industry bodies started giving up on "craft beer" in favour of the simpler and more containable principle of independent ownership, I decided the genuine feelings and associations behind the term "craft beer" – the feelings and associations that had inspired such passionate argument – were too important to give up on.

And so, this project evolved from a chat, into a conference presentation, then into what was going to be a long essay, and finally into a full-on book.

Turns out I am that predictable after all.

As is the case with many books, I spent months talking about this project instead of writing it. The idea is too niche for the people who usually publish my books, so I made plans to self-publish it as something that was, in the words of every music press interview with an up-and-coming band, primarily for my own enjoyment, and if anyone else liked it, that would be a bonus.

And then Coronavirus happened.

I'm writing these words eleven weeks after I last left my house. I have no idea when I will again. In my last week of normal life, I travelled to various beer events up and down the UK, giving some of those talks I love so much, and spending time with passionate craft brewers and drinkers, all while witnessing the build-up to what was to come, a gradual unravelling of normality that simultaneously felt like it was accelerating by the day, and slowing everything to an imminent halt. First, hand sanitiser, then toilet roll disappeared from the shelves. People went from joking about social distancing and coming up with ironic takes on the new elbow bump gesture that had replaced handshakes, to looking genuinely scared. After the last conference, I spent the first two weeks home in quarantine, because my wife is high-risk thanks to a lung condition, and people who I had drunk with days before had developed full-blown Covid-19. As the virus progressed, it also emerged that overweight men in their fifties with hypertension fare a lot worse than most if we contract the disease. Luckily, I have a well-stocked beer cellar. Or at least, I did eleven weeks ago.

Liz and I both work for ourselves, and I do so in the hospitality industry, which was shut down a week before everything else. Our work evaporated into nothing. With no income, and no structure to our lives in this terrifying time, I hatched a plan to write and self-publish this book within 13 weeks, with Liz working as editor, publisher and researcher. She's always done the first read and edit on my books before I send them to my publisher, and this time she got to finish the job. When I shared the idea on social media, asking if people would be prepared to buy a book like this and what they might pay for it, the reaction was overwhelming. So, if you're reading this at some point in the future when normality has returned, this is what we did during Coronavirus lockdown. It kept us safe and sane. I hope you got through it OK too.

At the time of writing, we have no idea what long-term impact lockdown and social distancing will have on the craft beer movement – all we know is that it's going to be significant. I face a daily choice between being optimistic and pessimistic about this. On my optimistic days, I believe that, at least in the medium-term, some of the underlying ideas and beliefs discussed in this book will become more important to us than ever, and that this will help craft breweries bounce back and thrive once more.

Most of my books follow a rough narrative thread. This one works in a slightly different way. It's not trying to be an academic analysis of its subject, because I'm not an academic, but it leans on a lot of work that is, and it has ended up developing a structure that echoes some of those books. It's an argument rather than a story, and it falls into three parts.

In Part One – "Craft beer is completely undefinable" – we'll look at how the unstoppable force of craft beer hit the immovable tangle of paradox, confusion, obfuscation, passion, prejudice and cynicism about the need to define what it actually is. Next, we'll explore the origins of the term "craft beer", look at the various attempts to give it an "official" concrete definition, and explain why these have failed, concluding that a concrete, measurable definition of craft beer is impossible. We'll see that as a result, the term "craft beer" is in the process of being abandoned by what most of us still think of as the craft brewing industry, in favour of something more concrete and defensible, but far less evocative. This does leave the maligned term "craft beer" at something of a loose end, setting the scene for an argument for why it should be saved and rehabilitated rather than quietly forgotten, like "microbrewery" was before it, even if it cannot be defined in measurable terms.

Part Two – "Craft beer is hopelessly misunderstood" – forms the bulk of the book. Here, we'll put beer aside for a bit, picking it up for just an occasional swig as we look at the term "craft" in its broadest sense, the origins of the word, and how it was applied over centuries before it ever became conjoined with the word "beer". We'll explore what "craft" means, and why we care so much about it. We'll focus on three periods in history: the industrialisation of work in the nineteenth century; the automation of work and the growth of huge corporations in the 1970s; and the transformation of society in the early 21st century, by algorithms, high-speed mobile computing and the arrival of artificial intelligence. We'll explore how the creeping conformity and commodification of every aspect of our lives generated the current interest in craft, both in beer and in a much broader sense, and show why "craft beer" belongs absolutely at the centre of this broader notion of craft.

In Part Three - "Craft beer is absolutely essential" - we'll build the idea of craft beer back up again, from the perspective you get when you actually look at the "craft" part as much as the "beer" part. We'll suggest four pillars around which the meaning should be built: Skill and Creativity (yes that's two things but it's one pillar); Quality (which may be a corollary of skill but remains a different pillar); Autonomy, and Motivation. We will happily demonstrate that these four pillars can in no way form the basis of a measurable, quantifiable definition, and then argue that this doesn't matter, because "craft beer" remains a meaningful, relevant and appealing concept whether it has a measurable definition or not.

I'm sure none of this will be controversial at all.

I'd like to thank Liz Vater for being my co-creator on this project in every way possible. Thanks also to Marian Broderick who provided an invaluable steer on the edit and structure. For help, guidance and support, thank you to Stephen Beaumont, Chris Gittner, Emmanuel Gobillot, Emma Inch, Matt Kirkegaard, Kate Manning, Rachel McCormack, Daniel Nielson, Garrett Oliver, Evan Rail, Adrian Tierney-Jones, Tom Thurnell-Read, and all the fans of beer and of my writing who made me believe this project was both possible and worthwhile, for astounding me with your kindness and encouragement.

Whatever you thought this book was going to be when you bought it, this probably isn't it. On the road towards our destination of making sense of craft beer, we'll detour via woodwork, wallpaper and glass-blowing, and examine the appeal of Renaissance philosophy, digging, macramé, open-plan offices and Felicity Kendal. We'll be torturing an analogy with Sid Meier's *Civilization* video games half to death, arguing that the 1970s British TV programme *Play School* gave those of us who watched it as kids a taste of life in North Korea, and briefly ponder whether there is any such thing as language. You will no doubt become angry with me at some points, and if you have taken any position at all on the craft beer debate before now, you will certainly disagree with at least some of what I have to say. But please don't throw your Kindle across the room – it was probably expensive. Get yourself a beer, and strap in: it's going to be a bumpy ride.

Cheers,

Pete Brown
Lockdown London, May 2020

Part One:
"Craft Beer" is completely undefinable

Chapter 1:
"It's got more artisan in it"

Given the contrarian nature of this exercise, why don't we start this exploration of craft beer with a story about cider?

When craft beer exploded into the UK mainstream in the mid-2010s, "craft cider" was conspicuous by its absence as a running mate. Cider had enjoyed a global explosion of interest about a decade previously, and the effects of that boom were now quickly wearing off, as rapid volume growth settled down into another period of stagnation. Meanwhile, beer – which had been stagnant and boring itself for a long while – was now being given a massive adrenaline shot to the heart by the craft beer boom. For people like me, who were writing about both beer and cider at the time, the parallels seemed obvious: why was no one making any noise about craft cider? There were plenty of ciders around that, in my opinion, could happily and proudly be called that, but no one – neither cider makers nor industry marketers nor drinkers – seemed interested in doing so. That is, not until a blustery Thursday afternoon in the early spring of 2015.

In the British cider market, between the handful of large corporations mass-producing cider in factories, and the hundreds of small-scale cider makers who are mostly farm-based and serve local markets, there exists a growing number of companies who were also small-scale and farm-based as recently as twenty or thirty years ago, but have grown to a level where they are now nationally available in pubs and supermarkets. Some are even being advertised on TV. The older drinkers you still find in cider barns around Somerset or Herefordshire will happily bend your ear about how they can remember the days when Old Man _____ still made the cider himself, before the young 'uns took over and brought in these fancy new ideas, and how it was good cider back then, some of the best, but now they've dumbed it down for the supermarkets and you can't even call it cider no more.

Depending on which market data analyst you speak to, these are the "premium" or even "super-premium" ciders that supposedly sit at the top of the mainstream market – Weston's, Aspall and Thatcher's being the best-known. They're the ciders I would usually choose to drink before I met photographer Bill Bradshaw and co-wrote *World's Best Cider* (2013) with him, and I still find many of them acceptable today. Some are very good indeed, even if, as a proper cider aficionado, you're not supposed to say that.

Every year, a couple of these cider makers host market briefings for drinks writers such as myself, in which they present a run-down of stats and data on how cider is doing as a product category, followed by their latest news.

One year, one of these cider brands used their briefing to launch a new "craft cider". It was packaged in 330ml (11 US fl oz) cans, with a bright, stencilled, type-led design. It had borrowed these visual cues from craft beer, and was unashamedly appealing to that audience. It looked great.

The story we were told about the cider inside the can was that, being craft, it was produced in small batches by an independent cider maker, had its own authentic provenance, and boasted a full, uncompromising flavour.

That's a fair enough attempt to set out the stall of what a "craft cider" should be. But it's also a perfect description of pretty much every small-scale farmhouse cider in the UK, including several ciders made by the same company that was here launching their "first craft cider". Why was this new canned cider "craft" when all these other ciders, by implication, were not?

It was an obvious question, and it wasn't long before it was asked by one of the journalists in the room. The presenter knew far more about public relations than she did about cider making, because that was her job. She was clearly flummoxed. She didn't give a satisfying answer, because she didn't really understand the question, so different members of the audience chipped in and expanded upon it, asking it in different ways. Traditional farmhouse cider is made on a small scale, using traditional ingredients and processes, and has an uncompromised and uncompromising flavour. You could, if you wanted, surely refer to that as craft cider. So why bother launching a new cider in a can rather than just redefining what you had?

Finally, the presenter pointed to the can in her hand, and said, "This one has got more artisan in it."

To be fair, she did come up with that on the spot, under growing pressure. That's what good PRs do.

Just to make it perfectly clear, "artisan" is not an ingredient, like apple juice or sugar, that can be added to a fermentation vat. Perhaps she meant to say, "This one is more artisanal," which is a word that's often bandied around as a synonym for craft, and is preferable to some simply because it doesn't carry as much baggage as "craft" now does.

The reason for bringing up this story now is not to make fun of the poor PR. "This one has got more artisan in it" isn't even the most stupid thing I've ever heard in conversations about defining craft drinks, though it is on the medals podium.

The story is relevant because long after this launch event, the company was still referring to this product as its first "craft cider." But the only thing that made it any different from the other independently-owned, authentic, full-flavoured ciders the company made was that this one came in a really cool-looking can.

Traditional small-scale farmhouse cider is often packaged in plastic flagons with really bad label design or, sometimes, with no label at all, just the name of the cider scrawled in wobbly Sharpie.

What everyone in the room was thinking, and what the company was implying, was that if a full-flavoured, small-batch, authentic product comes in cool packaging, it is craft. If it doesn't, it's not. If you think about the word "craft" in any context other than alcoholic drinks, then whatever associations that word evokes in its own right, I'm betting my house that "really cool, contemporary packaging design" is not one of them.

The makers of the "first craft cider" were guilty only of taking their cues from the craft beer market – and who can blame them? Craft beer is a multi-billion-dollar global industry that has shaken the overall beer market to its foundations, totally transforming its shape. For five years running, from 2014 to 2018, craft beer was cited in an annual survey of business leaders in the British hospitality industry as the most influential trend across all drinks in the UK.[1] If I were a medium-sized cider maker, I'd be looking to learn whatever I could from that.

So who drinks craft beer?

If we switch our perspective from business analysis to the people who actually drink it – which the industry doesn't do enough of – then it makes sense to divide craft beer fans into three roughly-defined concentric circles. To the inner circle, the most hardcore craft beer fans, this is not just a beer choice; it's a movement and lifestyle, with its own

---

[1] CGA Business Leader Surveys 2014-2018. Craft was knocked off the top spot in 2019 by low- and no-alcohol beers – the growth of which has been driven to a large extent by craft beer.
https://www.cga.co.uk/all-reports/business-leaders-survey-report-2019/

language, dress code, ethics and conventions. Brewers, retailers, bloggers, wholesalers and devoted fans connect in a global scene where many of the relationships are personal and face-to-face, or at least, smartphone-to-smartphone.

The second circle outside the core gives craft beer the "hipster" associations it only partially deserves. For a certain breed of image-conscious young person, beer has replaced alternative music as the main touchstone around which to define a style tribe: eight years go, in the hipster-centric part of North London where I live, the tribal uniform included T-shirts emblazoned with classic album covers from the likes of Led Zeppelin, Sonic Youth and Joy Division (often worn by people who had never heard the album, or were even aware that the image was an album cover in the first place.) Now, these have been largely replaced by hoodies bearing the logos of local microbreweries.

Finally, to the biggest circle – taking us to around 24 million people in the UK, last time I checked[2] – "craft beer" is simply a drink they consume regularly. They may not know exactly what makes it different, or "craft", but they're rapidly discovering their favourite hop variety in a way their parents began to discern the difference between Chardonnay and Sauvignon Blanc grapes in the late 1990s.

So craft beer is big business. But we can also see from these pen-portraits that its success is bound up with a lot more than citrusy hops. There's a big image dimension in play too, something which the die-hard craft fan is often reluctant to accept. Image-based marketing is what the mainstream does. It's inauthentic and mediated. If you're into craft, that's because you only care about what's on the

---

[2]Marston's *On-Trade Beer Report 2019* (https://www.marstons.co.uk/docs/reports/2019/on-trade-beer-report-2019.pdf) cites survey research conducted by Eureka showing that 58% of all beer drinkers claim to "understand what craft beer is, and drink it." Grossed up to represent the population at large, this equates to just under 24 million people.

inside.

Yeah, right. If that were true, how come the cider guys could analyse craft beer's success, and conclude that the best way they could enjoy a piece of the action was to put some cider in a really cool-looking can?

It's all about authenticity, except when it's "real"

The "first craft cider" is important because the company was looking towards craft beer at a time when the aluminium can had somehow gone from being seen as the cheapest, most downmarket format in which to buy beer, to becoming the most premium, in the space of five years. There are some sound, ecological and product quality reasons for this[3], but these have always been true of the aluminium can. What changed was that craft brewers made aluminium cans look cool, upending market convention. In any field, whenever a group of upstarts seeks to take control of the narrative, reversing established norms is part of the playbook, challenging conceptions of what is aspirational, what is normal, and what is unacceptable.

But starting our story with the parallel of cider's look towards beer to learn how to break market rules is important for an additional reason: in the UK, beer had its own version of that shitty plastic flagon with the name scribbled on in Sharpie.

The modern craft beer movement is primarily associated with the United States. When it emerged there, it did so against a background in which interesting, flavourful beer had been completely wiped out. American beer was the butt

---

[3]Cans are lighter and therefore more energy-efficient to transport. They stack better. They're more easily recyclable. And they keep beer fresher for longer by keeping out the degenerative effects of UV light. But boy, do they look cool too.

of a global joke about making love in a canoe. If you got a flavourful, interesting beer in the US in the late 1970s or early 1980s, then unless it was from the exception that proved the rule that was San Francisco's Anchor Brewery, it was either from a brand-new start-up or it was imported.

The UK was different. While bland, industrial, fake-pilsner lagers were reaching the same level of dominance here that they'd achieved globally a century before, we still had cask ale, known more colloquially as real ale. The Campaign for Real Ale (CAMRA) had fought a successful rear-guard action to stop this traditional British beer style from disappearing.

If cask ale hadn't existed before now, it would be a hipster's wet dream. Its close or even distant equivalents in any other sphere of food and drink apart from beer are lionised.

Don't get me wrong: I love a great wine. I like the sense of theatre where the sommelier has to carefully open the bottle, sniff the cork, pour a bit of the wine, swirl it and ask you to taste it – this is a genuine skill that is not to be sniffed at (sorry). But imagine if that world-class sommelier had to take delivery of that world-class wine and then tamper with it in the cellar because it wasn't quite finished, and the skill of the sommelier themselves was a key part of whether the wine was great or awful when it hit the glass?

A great bottle of red has to breathe for a while when it's been opened. A great barrel of cask ale has to be stillaged at the right temperature for several days. It still contains live yeast, which has been dormant since the beer flowed into the cask. It would taste pretty good if you sampled it at this stage, but it wouldn't taste right. Once the beer is comfortable in the pub cellar, it is tapped and vented – a hole is punched on the top to allow air in, and the oxygen acts like a dose of smelling salts to the dormant yeast. It rouses itself, and starts a sluggish, secondary fermentation in the cask. This slow secondary fermentation doesn't increase the alcohol by much, but it provides a natural sparkle of carbon dioxide, and it completes the flavours in the beer, knitting them together to create a smoothness and mellowness that gives traditional British beer a depth and complexity of character at a lower level of alcohol than you'll find in any other beer in the world. If cask ale had had its origins in a French or Italian tradition rather than a British one, Michelin-starred restaurants around the world would no doubt be rated on their ability to cellar ale properly as well as their ability to buy and stock a nice bottle of wine.

Most beer is filtered and pasteurised before being packaged in pressurised kegs, and is artificially carbonated. This makes it more reliable and easier to handle, and is therefore the draft packaging format used by mass-market beers. It's perfectly possible to produce outstanding beers in this format – in fact some craft beer styles are more suited to it than to cask – but because it was for so long synonymous with bland, gassy beers, "keg" became the enemy of the card-carrying cask devotee. The lines between the two are much blurred now thanks to craft brewers innovating with unpasteurised and unfiltered keg products, but cask versus keg is a debate that still rages inside beer aficionado bubbles.

Whatever your views on keg – assuming you have any at all – cask beer is a distinct speciality that deserves to be celebrated. But we Brits simply haven't figured out a way of being proud of our food and drink traditions without sounding like we want to storm the Reichstag. So while people who really love their food and drink "get" cask ale, some of its most vocal fans revert to blurting "It's British", "It's proper", or "It's traditional" when asked why anyone should care about it. Indulge that attitude too far, and you may find that it comes with a free side-order of rejecting "filthy foreign muck." While that risk is lower now than it was, by its nature, cask ale – identifiable by its tall wooden handpumps rather than the chilled, brightly-lit, gas-assisted fonts serving filtered and pasteurised keg beers – tends to be aligned in popular imagination with attitudes that are reactionary rather than progressive.

So when the American craft beer influence arrived in the UK, the two felt very different. British real ale looked backward and inward, preserving an old tradition that had been in danger of disappearing. American craft beer had no tradition left to save, so it looked forward and outward, taking inspiration from wherever it could to create something new. As it became established in the UK in the early 2010s, American craft beer looked young, fresh, energetic and cool, while good old British cask ale looked old, fusty, traditional and boring. Additionally, the flavours in US craft were bolder and brasher, while the flavours in British cask were subtler and more delicate. While there are many drinkers who appreciate both, there were also fans of one that were hostile to the other: two rival groups of beardy, geeky obsessives each calling out the other as the enemy of good beer.

Just as farmhouse cider is not considered craft, for many, neither is traditional British cask ale. Many cask ale fans don't want to be associated with the word, which they see as a meaningless marketing slogan (I've got news for you there, guys: "real ale" is just as much of an invented marketing slogan, first coined just over a decade before "craft beer".) Fans of craft beer fire back that real ale could never be craft beer even if they wanted it to be, because it's so boring, twiggy and *old*.

You might think that the people involved in brewing and selling cask ale and craft beer would want to clear up any conflict between the two, especially as many small, independent breweries now produce both. But this is not so. The modern craft beer phenomenon emerged from outside the traditional British brewing industry, so elements of that industry have been uncertain how to define it or how to treat it. Market analysts CGA audit sales through pubs, and when they classify which brands belong where, they look at ales brand-by-brand to decide whether or not they are "craft", using a number of criteria including price point, what kinds of places it's sold in, what kind of bottle or can it comes in, and whether or not the branding looks modern or not.[4] Marston's Brewery, which produces comprehensive annual guides to beer's performance in the UK on-trade and off-trade, ran a piece of research in 2019 asking drinkers to name a craft beer brand. In the words of the report, 55% of respondents named "a brand more associated with traditional ale" (such as Ringwood's Thumper), while just 45% "*correctly* named a recognised craft brand" (my italics for emphasis) such as BrewDog or Brooklyn.[5] Those "traditional ales" are most readily associated with cask dispense, whereas craft brands are more strongly associated with keg.

It's important to note that the only people who were asked this question were those who had already said that they understood what craft beer was, and that they drank it. Survey after survey shows that both modern US-influenced craft beers and traditional British cask ales are considered by drinkers to be beers that are being brewed in smaller batches, to a higher quality standard, serving a more localised market, than industrial brewers. The majority of all those millions of craft beer drinkers don't seem to care whether the brewer is an old and traditional one that probably puts its beer out in cask, or young and funky and relying on kegs and cans. Yet the people who ran the Marston's survey are implying that people are mistaken if they think "craft" applies to traditional cask ale brands. That broad mass of drinkers in our third circle may not care, but the industry and its superfans really do.

This particular conundrum over the definition and meaning

---

[4]https://www.morningadvertiser.co.uk/Article/2019/01/25/How-is-craft-beer-defined
[5]http://www.marstons.co.uk/docs/reports/2018/on-trade-beer-report-2018.pdf

of craft doesn't really need any further absurdities heaped upon it, but at the risk of causing PTSD for both myself and any veterans of the craft debate, I'm going to give them to you anyway. Firstly, until 2014, "traditional" was one of three criteria used by the American Brewers' Association (BA) to define "craft beer". And secondly, talk to the founding fathers of the cool, funky American craft breweries that British craft beer geeks love so much, and they will tell you without hesitation that the beers that inspired them to give up good jobs and set up small breweries instead were... any guesses? Yep... traditional British cask ales. When I blogged about this in 2018, Garrett Oliver, the Brewmaster of Brooklyn Brewery, who trained as a brewer in England, responded in the comments, "I've heard British craft brewers talking about 'Fuller's isn't craft' and 'Sierra Nevada isn't craft'. These people are out of their minds. American craft beer culture is BASED on what we went and saw in the UK, Germany and Belgium. Everyone on earth copied everything from Fuller's ESB to Duvel, and they have the gall to say that these breweries aren't craft breweries?"

So, to sum up: in the eyes of both British craft beer drinkers and large parts of the British brewing establishment, traditional British real ales are *not* craft beers, and modern American beers *are* craft beers, even though the American definition of craft beer for a long time said that "traditional" was an important part of what defines craft beer, and the American craft beers we all love so much began life as homages to the non-craft traditional British beers that a majority of British craft beer drinkers mistakenly believe to be craft beers, like the brewers of American craft beers do.

All clear? Good. Because you may be surprised to hear that it can get a bit confusing when you try to apply these rules to the everyday reality of British brewing.

The blog I wrote, to which Garrett responded, was inspired by the sale of Dark Star, a craft brewery in Sussex that was one of the pioneers of brewing with American hops in the UK, to traditional London brewer Fuller's. This prompted an online discussion as to whether or not this meant Dark Star was still a craft brewer – or indeed, if it ever had been. The clear implication was that Fuller's was not a craft brewery. Those who believed Dark Star never had been based that opinion on the fact that the smaller brewer packaged its beers mainly in cask.

This led me to muse on the specifics. Let's say a small, independent brewery produces beer across a variety of formats. What percentage of its total output is allowed to be cask ale before it no longer counts as a craft brewery? If that brewery packages beer in kegs, casks, cans and bottles, are its kegs and cans craft and its cask beers not craft? Where do bottles fit in?[6] If, say, Thornbridge brews a batch of an American-influenced IPA called Jaipur, and puts some into cask and some into keg, is the cask stuff not craft while the keg stuff is? If the cask Jaipur is not craft but the keg Jaipur is craft, how does that work? Does Jaipur start off as a craft beer in the brewhouse, and when the cask stuff gets packaged into the cask it stops being craft? Or is it the other way around: Jaipur starts off *not* being craft, but when the keg stuff gets packaged into kegs, that's when it becomes craft? What is it about the cask process/format that stops it from being craft? Is it the live yeast, which requires more skill, care and attention to look after? Is it the container itself, which is more traditional than a pressurised keg? Is it the shape of the cask? Or is it the sound of the word "cask", which simply doesn't ring with enough craftiness?

I could go on. But you'll be glad to hear that I've decided not to. Because this exercise in logical silliness is simply one example of the problems surrounding craft beer, a localised, British member of a family of definitional headaches that

---

[6]If you look after a beer range in a British supermarket, the general rule is that ales packaged in 500ml brown glass bottles are not craft, but ales packaged in smaller or different bottles are.

spreads around the globe.

Maybe if I close my eyes and put my hands over my ears, it'll go away

After surviving the absurdities of this initial skirmish with the definitional problems of craft beer, you can at least appreciate why some people might argue that the term is meaningless, without foundation, entirely subjective and therefore without worth. This is an understandable response to a debate that remains peculiarly unsatisfying for anyone who takes part in it. As beer writer Tom Acitelli wrote in 2015, "How to ruin an evening with a beer geek: (Step 1) Define 'craft beer' and 'craft brewer' using the industry standard. (Step 2) Yield nothing."[7]

So this would be a good point to step away, forget about it, and go and do a jigsaw instead. It's the point at which it verges on masochism to press on. It's a point I passed years ago.

The contention that the term "craft beer" is meaningless is itself meaningless. If we can't define something, the fault is with us, not with the thing we're trying to define. The lack of a tight, universally agreed definition doesn't make craft beer an imaginary concept. These beers are there. And the fact that they provoke argument about whether they're "craft" or not, and further argument about the precise nature of what unites them in common as "craft", means by definition that "craft beer" *does* exist and is *not* meaningless. If it didn't exist, there wouldn't be so much trouble trying to define what it is, would there?

As part of my degree in International Relations, I took the

[7]"The Craft Beer Definition That Launched A Thousand Arguments," *All About Beer* magazine, 18th September 2015: http://allaboutbeer.com/the-craft-beer-definition/

pilot year of the UK's first ever academic course studying terrorism. We spent the first five weeks discussing the definition of terrorism. It's a complex subject, a matter of perspective: white mass-shooters in the United States are typically characterised as crazed lone-wolf gunmen, whereas brown mass-shooters in the United States are terrorists, even if both shooters cite political, religious or race-based motives for their actions. As my course tutors tired of hearing, one man's terrorist is another man's freedom fighter, Nelson Mandela being the example most often quoted.[8] At the time of my course, there were 276 different, rival definitions of terrorism conceived by academics, researchers and political institutions. I'm sure there are many more now. "What is the definition of terrorism?" was a standard finals exam essay question. Good luck arguing that terrorism doesn't exist, or that it's a meaningless term.

The reason there were 276 definitions of terrorism, the reason it was the most reliable exam question, was that the search for a definition was a crucial part in understanding the issue. As the examples above show, if we can't define it, it can be abused. If freedom fighters can be persecuted as terrorists, and terrorists can be excused as freedom fighters, then our freedom itself is at risk. Okay, so craft beer may not be quite as important. But while there are many people who want a black and white definition of craft beer simply because they can't deal with shades of grey, the craft beer movement itself – the brewers whose livelihoods depend on it – seeks a definition to ensure its own survival. And with good reason.

We are Beer. You will be assimilated.

Craft beer rose up as a direct response to the actions of

---

[8]Mandela was described as a terrorist and a communist by Ronald Reagan and Margaret Thatcher in the 1980s. Now remembered as one of the greatest statesmen of modern times, Mandela remained on the United States terrorism watchlist until 2008.

large, corporate brewers who had destroyed much of what was great about beer and brewing. Starting in the late nineteenth century, when per capita consumption of beer peaked, the brewing industry became a battle for market share rather than absolute growth. Like the Great White Shark that will die if it stops swimming forward, shareholder-owned corporations must grow ever bigger – that's what they do. It's their nature. If they stop growing, their share price falls, and they become vulnerable to takeover. When they are taken over, the acquiring company is usually more interested in obtaining routes to market than specific beers, so the choice available to the consumer shrinks. All this merger and acquisition activity creates a thirst for cash. Beer is a mass-market, low-margin product. In a stagnant or declining market, cost-cutting becomes at least as important as revenue growth. So beer is made faster, with cheaper ingredients.

The drive, the obsession, of big brewers is to become or remain the market leader. That means having as many people liking your product as possible. And it is this, even more than the cheapening of the brewing process, that leads to blander beer. I've sat in focus groups where the respondents are tasting a new beer. Let's say three people think it's the best beer they have ever tasted, four say it's OK and they would probably drink it, and one really dislikes it because it tastes too bitter. The client would invariably come out of the group saying, "We need to make it less bitter."

"Why?"

"Because that one guy really hated it."

"Yes, but those other three really loved it."

"Doesn't matter. It's too bitter."

Big beer marketers often work on the assumption of a

hierarchy of consumer attitudes towards their brand. At the bottom you have "rejectors", and then one better than that is "non-rejectors". Some of these can be persuaded to like the brand more than tolerate it, and some of these can be persuaded to like it even more. This creates a pyramid (it's a fundamental law of business that marketers must have at least one pyramid in any PowerPoint deck) until at the apex, you have "adorers". Obviously, you want lots of adorers, but because each layer gets smaller as you go up, the logic is that you're only going to get a big layer at the top if you start off at the bottom with as many non-rejectors as you possibly can. That's why clients would have been happier with eight people in that focus group saying the beer was OK rather than three loving it and one hating it. And that's why mainstream beer gets blander and blander. In terms of absolute quality, it may even be technically superior to many craft beers. But it has been designed and engineered to offend no one.

In the late 1990s – ten years before craft beer exploded in the UK – I presented arguments to beer marketers showing that there was a small but affluent group of people who were curious about flavour and character and were willing to spend a bit more to get it. No, they argued, I was wrong. When it came to beer, people wanted it to be light and refreshing, and that was all. I pointed to examples from across the rest of food and drink, showing how tastes were becoming more adventurous. Wine was taking share from beer. Dark spirits were taking share from white. Ciabatta and wholemeal bread were taking from sliced white, and real coffee was taking from instant. Were these people really going to farmers' markets and deli counters and spending more than they had ever spent before on charcuterie, complicated salads and exotic vegetables, and then saying, "You know what? I'd love to wash all this down with a can of Foster's." I was told that beer was different, the only food or drink product of any kind where people were not interested in exploring better flavour or quality.

Craft beer – or more specifically, the beer styles that drive its growth – simply could not have happened within the structure and processes of a corporate brewing industry that has maximum market penetration and chronic fear of risk at its heart. The fundamental issue with basing marketing decisions on consumer research is that people can only respond to the questions they are asked and the concepts they are shown. None of those big brewers ever did a focus group where mainstream lager drinkers said in unison, "I wish there was a beer that had aromas of citrus, tropical fruit and pine resin, a solid malty back bone, and an assertive bitter finish," because they didn't know beer could be like that – no one had told them it could be. So in a circle of mediocrity, big brewers were never going to brew one.

Craft came along when beer was boring, stagnant, commoditised and disrespected. A handful of big brands dominated, and they all tasted pretty similarly of not very much. For decades, people "drank the advertising" – their affinity to a particular brand being driven by highly effective image-based marketing. But in the early 21st century, as advertising restrictions tightened in a climate of moral panic over "binge drinking," the great TV ads were stifled. With little in the way of product innovation, and marketing budgets increasingly being spent on price promotion instead of brand building, beer became one of the least thought-about, most routine choices of what went in the supermarket trolley. People who may have once been ferociously loyal to, say, Becks, and ideologically opposed to drinking Budweiser, would now drink whichever of the top brands had the best deal that week.

That's precisely why craft beer captured the imagination of the broader beer-drinking public. It was the biggest upheaval in the beer market since the repeal of prohibition in the US or the mass conversion to lager in the UK. And it happened *without the permission* of the handful of brewers who dominated the beer market in share terms and had a stranglehold over the channels of distribution. The growth of craft beer rejuvenated interest in beer worldwide, attracting and delighting people who previously believed they "didn't like" beer based on their impressions of mainstream lager. You want to see *real* adorers? Check out any craft beer festival, anywhere in the world.

The big brewers didn't like this one bit.

When I visited the Great American Beer Festival for the first time in 2006, I had a conversation with a craft brewer who had recently attended the American Beer Distributors Annual Convention. It took place in one of those vast hotels with sickly carpets, movable walls and a general atmosphere of coming adrift in time and space. The large corporate brewers had lavish stands staffed by models in the main conference rooms, and the few craft brewers in attendance were all squeezed into an out-of-the-way conservatory. A rep for one of the big companies was finding the event curiously quiet, with hardly any enquiries at his stand, so he went for a wander. When he stumbled upon the craft beer annex, he found that most of the wholesalers were trying to squeeze themselves into the cramped space. He grabbed one of them, and asked what the hell was going on. What kind of sales gimmick were these craft beer guys pulling? "It's simple," the wholesaler replied. "Your beer sells for three bucks a bottle. Theirs sells for four-fifty."

When it is threatened, Big Beer will initially attempt to dismiss or play down the threat. If this doesn't work, they will sow confusion, attacking the threat and deliberately trying to confuse the consumer over its nature and appeal. If that fails too, they'll buy the threat to negate it. Philip van Munching, whose grandfather founded the firm that imported and sold Heineken in the United States, termed it the "denigrate, regulate, replicate" strategy in *Beer Blast* (1997), his look at the history of beer marketing in America, and gave many examples of it being used to good effect.[9]

We saw a great example of it in the UK, around the same time the American craft beer movement was waking up to the need to defend itself from the corporate threat. From the start, the British lager market prized foreign provenance as a sign of sophistication. No matter what country you're in, imports are generally regarded as premium to domestic, and here in the UK, where we default to thinking that foreign food and drink is always superior to what we do, we took it to an absurd degree. In 1970, lager accounted for just seven per cent of all beer consumed in the UK. Ten years later, it had grown its share to thirty, and by 1990, it accounted for more than half the market. There are all sorts of reasons why lager didn't take off here until the 1970s, then grew so rapidly after that.[10] One of the main ones was that this was the decade foreign holidays went mass-market. Beer drinkers who had turned up their noses at lager in Britain discovered it was the only beer style available on beaches around the Mediterranean, and learned to like it a great deal. Back home, it was a reminder of sunny days and foreign adventures. Buy a foreign lager, and you weren't just drinking the product of a country; you were imbuing yourself with some of that country's character and culture.

Naturally, drinkers of these aspirational foreign beers were angry when they subsequently discovered they were actually drinking weaker versions of European beers like Heineken or Carlsberg that had been watered down for British tastes and were being brewed in places like Luton or Bedford. Brands such as Hofmeister and Skol were invented by British brewers and given foreign-sounding names, deliberately misleading drinkers over their origins, a trend

[9]Van Munching, Phillip: *Beer Blast: The Inside Story of the Brewing Industry's Bizarre Battles for Your Money,* (Times Business, New York, 1997) p.46.
[10]I discuss these reasons in great detail in my first book, *Man Walks into a Pub: A Sociable History of Beer* (Pan Macmillan, London, 2003).

that Warrington brewer Greenall Whitley took to its piss-taking conclusion with its launch of Grunhalle lager. Lager drinkers felt betrayed, but – in a common and repeating pattern – only because they were aspiring to something the big brewers had taught them to desire in the first place.

So the big brewers responded by launching "export" and "premium" versions of these "standard" or "cooking" lagers. These were the real deal, the same beers that people drank in their country of origin and across Europe. Except it turned out that the tiny caption towards the end of the ads saying "Brewed in the EU" was masking the fact that these beers were still being brewed in factories close to provincial British motorways.

In the late 1990s I was working in an ad agency on the Stella Artois account. Stella was being brewed in its place of origin (the town of Leuven in Belgium) as well as in France, and two locations in the UK: Samlesbury in Lancashire, and Magor in South Wales. People wanted to drink "proper French Stella" instead of the UK stuff, even though the beer brewed in France was no more authentic than that brewed in Wales. So we did a blind taste test of Leuven, Magor, Salmesbury and French Stella. The differences between them were so small they were statistically irrelevant. But that's not what people were buying: they wanted their beer to come from the country they had been told it came from. And the ads we were making for Stella at the time strongly suggested, for reasons too complex to go into here, that it had its roots in the south of France.

Budweiser Budvar – the Czech one, not the beer that began life as an American copy of the style – has only ever been brewed in Ceske Budejovice in South Bohemia. The brewery's UK office was frustrated that big lager brands were falsely passing themselves off as being imported from continental Europe when Budvar was one of the few brands genuinely going to all the trouble of doing so. In the early 2000s, Budvar launched the category of "world beer" as an attempt to create a distinction between premium lagers brewed under licence in the UK and genuine imports. For a while, this had some traction and created buzz in the industry. But the term wasn't legally enforceable, so the big brewers simply adopted it and started calling beers like San Miguel (brewed in Northampton) and Staropramen (Burton-on-Trent) "world beer" as well. When they did this volubly enough, the drinks trade press went along with them, and the term quickly lost its original meaning. It's still used by the industry today as a category to try to create yet another premium level above "premium". But if its meaning is now unclear to the typical lager drinker, then perhaps that was Big Beer's intention all along.

A few years later, craft beer initially proved to be more resilient to the "denigrate, regulate, replicate" strategy than World Beer had. Big brewers couldn't get rid of it: its meaning and popularity only grew in the minds of beer drinkers, until by 2010, it was going mainstream. They put slogans like "crafted to refresh" on cans of Foster's lager, and ran poster ads claiming Stella Artois came from "the largest microbrewery in the world: Belgium". Still, craft beer surged while big lager floundered. So they launched beers like Shocktop in the US and Blue Moon around the world, beers that looked like craft beers but were in fact brewed by the same big corporations in the same big factories as Budweiser and Miller. And eventually, from around 2011 onwards, Big Beer simply began assimilating, Borg-like, some of the brewers who had risen against them.

I should say at this point that, in principle, I have absolutely no problem with big brewers creating excellent craft beers, should they want to. I'm actually delighted that Heineken, Carlsberg and AB-InBev are now all the owners and brewers of hoppy IPAs, proper craft lagers and barrel-aged stouts, some of which number among my favourite beers. In the late 1990s I was trying to persuade brewers to brew something more interesting than bland, insipid lagers. If one of those corporations now said, "Hey, Pete, turns out you were right. It may have taken us a while, but we're now creating interesting, flavourful beers just like you said we should," I'd sound a tad unreasonable if I replied, "No! How dare you? You're the big nasty guys! You're not supposed to brew good beer!"

The marketers and strategists working for big brewers wouldn't be doing their jobs properly if they weren't coming after craft. By all means resent them for doing so, but in their position, you would do the same, or you would be fired. In a beer market that is declining or at best stagnant, craft is creating all the noise, despite its small overall market share. Any business with sense is going to want a piece of that action.

Also, we should remember that big brewers are capable of brewing beers of outstanding technical quality, even if they taste of nothing. I've lost count of the number of craft brewers who hate Budweiser and all it stands for, yet still praise it as an extraordinary achievement of brewing skill: it takes real talent to make so many millions of bottles of beer, brewed in twelve different locations around the US plus many more around the world, using ingredients that vary in character from one harvest to the next, all taste bland and insipid in *exactly* the same way, time after time.

I enjoy the facetiousness of that insight. But it's also worth considering that big brewers have bigger budgets and therefore better access to the latest technology. When I met Brett Porter, Brewmaster at Goose Island in Chicago in 2014, I asked the inevitable question about the quality and integrity of Goose Island IPA now it was being brewed at a large Budweiser brewery in Fort Collins. He responded by telling me that the bottling line in the old brewery was over twenty years old and simply not up to scratch any more, that they had an issue with oxygen getting into the bottles and shortening the beer's shelf life. The bottling line at the Budweiser brewery was state-of-the-art, built to a spec that a small craft brewer would never be able to afford, so in that particular aspect, the beer was better quality than it ever had been or ever could be at the small, artisanal brewery where it was born. When I spoke to Alastair Hook, founder of London's Meantime Brewing, shortly after they had been taken over by what was then SABMiller, he was delighted that they'd bought him a gas chromatograph for cutting-edge analysis of the properties of hops – something that remained out of his price range while he was on his own.

If big brewers make it clear where the beer has come from, and what kind of company has brewed it, then as a beer drinker I really can't object.

But that is a very big "if".

It's not enough for some companies to have greater economies of scale, bigger budgets and control over routes to market: on top of that, they have to play dirty too. Actively choosing to buy from small, independent brewers may not be a key motivation for people who enjoy a pint of craft beer every now and then as a change from Carling, Castle or Castlemaine, but it matters a great deal to the early adopters who helped craft beer grow to the point where the mainstream drinker began to notice it. These people want to know where their beer is from and who made it, and if you think it's okay to deceive them or withhold that information from them, you're no better than a cheap carnival conman, no matter how sharp your suit or expensive your Rolex might be.

Even if we are happy drinking flavourful beers from bigger brewers, it's still the small, independent brewers who provide forward motion in the beer world. They are nimble and adaptable, can experiment and innovate in a fraction of the time Big Beer can, basing their decisions on what beers they want to brew and drink rather than maximising the number of non-rejectors in focus groups. As such, they bring back to beer a sense of dynamism and momentum it lost long ago. The independent craft brewing sector is vital to the health of the entire global beer industry. If big brewers fail to see that, then the small independent sector is not just protecting itself – it's protecting big brewers from their own rapacious nature too.

And so we persist.

As drinkers, we *want* "craft beer" to mean something, and as an industry, small, independent craft brewers *need* it to mean something. So it's not surprising that stakeholders and followers of the craft beer revolution want a clear, precise definition of what they are drinking, brewing, buying, loving, geeking out over and talking about.

Not surprising but, as we'll see in the next chapter, ultimately futile.

Chapter 2:
"Traditional or innovative"

It's commonly understood that craft beer originated as an American concept. As is often the case, the common understanding is wrong.

Before the words "craft" and "beer" were roped together in an attempt to create a definitional term, the words "craft" and "crafted" already had a long history in and around the brewing industry. Beer writers Boak & Bailey give a comprehensive overview of early uses of these terms in *Beer Britannia* (2014).[11] Debates over whether brewing was an art, a craft or a science, or a bit of all three, stretch back at least to the mid-nineteenth century. Burton brewer Worthington's was talking about "the craft of brewing" in advertisements in the 1930s.

But there's a big difference between talking about brewing as a craft or beers as being crafted, and creating the term "craft beer". Rather than talking about the discipline of brewing in general as a craft, when we designate some specific beers as craft beers, we are attempting to create a distinction between different types of beer, suggesting that some beers are crafted and others are not, or at least that some beers are more crafted than others. This is a distinction that was not made until recently – although perhaps not as recently as you might think.

The more you study beer writing, the more you realise that the trail-blazing beer writer Michael Jackson did everything first. He invented beer styles, he invented beer tasting notes,

---

[11]Boak, Jessica, and Bailey, Ray, *Beer Britannia*: The Strange Rebirth of British Beer, (Aurum, London, 2014) pp183-4.

he was the first English speaker to write about the Belgian beer scene and probably saved its life as a result, popularising it around the world. So it should come as no surprise to any beer fan that Jackson was also talking about "craft brewing" years before anyone else. In his seminal 1977 *World Guide to Beer*, he uses the terms "craft-brewer" and "craft-brewed" to refer to brewers in the USA, Belgium and France who were creating good beers in a fashion that contrasted from industrial breweries.[12] Boak & Bailey argue that he was probably looking for the closest translation of the French *artisanale*. I think he was perhaps searching for a term to suggest to an audience of British beer lovers that "real ale", which had recently been coined by CAMRA and subsequently raised as a standard behind which lovers of interesting, flavourful beer could rally, was not the only brewing tradition in the world that was worth caring about. Either way, Jackson made no attempt to define what a "craft-brewer" was – and he was a writer who was very particular about his careful, patient, precise definitions. In using the term, he seemed to think its meaning was self-evident and needed no explanation.

In 1982, in the first edition of his *Pocket Guide to Beer*, Jackson gave the following entry for Timothy Taylor's, brewers of the legendary Landlord:

> TIMOTHY TAYLOR, Keighley [in Yorkshire, northern England]. A craft brewery down to the last detail. Very small, producing a wide range of all-malt beers on the edge of the moorland Brontë country. All the draught is cask-conditioned, and the bottled ale is unpasteurized.[13]

Gary Gillman, who unearthed this mention and shared it on his blog[14], argues that "with striking concision [Jackson]

---

[12]Jackson, Michael, *World Guide to Beer* (Quarto, London, 1977) pp179-80 and p204.
[13]Jackson, Michael, *The Simon & Schuster Pocket Guide to Beer* (1st edition, Simon & Schuster, New York, 1991) p81.
[14]http://www.beeretseq.com/first-use-of-term-craft-brewery/

defined keynotes of the beer renaissance for the next 30 years and coined its trademark phrase 'craft brewery'".

Gillman also leads us to passages in the same book where Jackson praises Belgian brewer Dupont for "demonstrating outstanding skills on the craft of top-fermentation" and explains that he retains his maximum five-star rating for breweries that share "dedication to an elusive craft".

Gillman is right to say that Jackson is clearly using the term as "a signifier of quality and (typically, or often at least) of small-scale brewing". But Jackson still leaves us in a space somewhere between using "crafted" as a way to evoke practices and approaches some brewers have, versus "craft" as a label that creates a distinct, measurable category which specifically includes some brewers and excludes others. The first to deliberately attempt the latter was American beer writer Vince Cottone.

Cottone's definition of craft beer faded from view long ago, to be supplanted by the "official" definition from the BA. But it contains all the issues we still discuss when we argue about craft beer (with one crucial exception) and therefore gives us a useful structure to explore the meaning – or otherwise – of the term. But before we do so, it's worth taking a brief look at why Cottone chose the c-word, and the context in which he did so.

When America endured prohibition for thirteen years, only a fraction of its breweries survived. When they reopened, they found an audience that had largely forgotten the bitter taste of beer and had been making do with sweet soft drinks instead. The character of American beer – which had previously majored in authentic German lager styles – became increasingly bland and tasteless. It's hard to remember now, but when I first started writing about beer in the early 2000s, my friends would laugh in disbelief when I told them I was drinking American beer.

49

The super-aggressive marketing of the 1970s "Beer Wars" wiped out swathes more American breweries who couldn't afford to keep up with the ad-spend arms race: by the mid-1970s, only a handful of breweries remained, the biggest grown fat and bloated on the spoils of victory, proudly boasting about the lack of character in their beers with slogans like "Everything you want from a beer – and less".[15]

The tide began to turn in 1976, when congressional legislation reduced the duty payable on the first 60,000 barrels a brewery produced from $9 to $7, provided its total output didn't exceed two million barrels. This gave a lifeline to small-scale brewers, a way of competing with the massive economies of scale of the big corporations. When the legislation was passed, there were hardly any breweries of that size to take advantage of it. But the number began to grow. In 1978, the US government also legalised home brewing, which had remained illegal under a footnote of prohibition that no one had quite got around to repealing. Beer lovers brewing in their garages soon found they would rather be doing this than the day job, and took advantage of the tax cut to make small-scale, local brewing a viable business.

This nascent brewing revival began to attract the attention of newspaper journalists, and when they wrote about it, they coined the term "microbreweries". This didn't feel satisfying to the players on the scene at the time. An obvious objection was that the brewer was being defined solely in terms of its size (a headache that would later came back to haunt craft beer). But a bigger objection was that it reminded people of "microcomputers", which is how the first generation of personal computers were being referred to at the time. The promise "microchips" made of a sci-fi future evoked a look and feel that was the opposite of everything these small, homespun brewers were aiming for.

---

[15]The strapline for the launch of Miller Lite in 1975.

Looking for an alternative, they tried terms like "nano-brewery" or "boutique brewery", but nothing quite seemed to fit. In 1984, Vince Cottone wrote an article in which he expressed frustration with the inadequacy of describing this new wave of breweries simply in terms of their size. In an article titled "Craft Brewing Comes of Age", he wrote:

> Perhaps a better definition of the breweries who make traditional, handmade beer in small batches primarily for local sale and local consumption would be "craft breweries" instead of the currently popular term "microbreweries".[16]

Two years later, in his book *Good Beer Guide: Breweries and Pubs of the Pacific Northwest*, Cottone expanded on his definition:

> I use the term Craft Brewery to describe a small brewery using traditional methods and ingredients to produce a handcrafted, uncompromised beer that is marketed locally. I refer to this beer as True Beer.[17]

It's a definition that's concise and clear. But it's not really a definition of craft beer at all – rather, it's a definition of the people or companies that make it. Up to this point, in discussing the definition of "craft beer", every mention we've found has talked about craft breweries rather than the beer itself. Cottone does go on to describe the beer as "True Beer", but his main interest is in defining the nature of the brewer that makes it.

This may seem like a trivial distinction, but it isn't. In 2012, in response to the growing number of big-brand beers adopting the style and imagery of the craft sector, the BA warned drinkers to beware of "crafty" beers that looked like

---

[16]*The New Brewer* magazine, Vol. 1, No. 5, September-October 1984, Brewers' Association.
[17]Cottone, Vince, *Good Beer Guide: Breweries and Pubs of the Pacific Northwest* (Homestead Book Company, Seattle, Washington, 1986.)

they were made by craft brewers but were not. The BA's Julia Herz insisted that the organisation does not define craft beer – it leaves that to the marketplace, adding, "No one should tell beer lovers what to drink".[18] But the whole "crafty" exercise contradicted this by its very existence, with BA communications clearly drawing a difference between "crafty beers" and "true craft beers" based on the size and ownership of the brewery that makes them. The BA is quite clear that any beer produced by any brewery that meets the definitional standard of a craft brewery is a craft beer, and any beer produced by a brewery that does not meet this definition is not a craft beer. We'll explore this in further detail, because it's a root cause of why we get confused over what craft beer is, and why craft has become a frustrating term to describe what we're talking about.

So, remembering that Vince Cottone is primarily defining a craft *brewer* and not a craft beer, let's come back to his definition and examine it in detail, breaking out the various key talking points that still persist when discussing and arguing over craft beer:

- Small scale
- Traditional methods and ingredients
- Made by hand
- Uncompromised
- Locally marketed

At the time of writing, not one of these criteria remain in the BA's definition of craft beer. The only key criterion that does – that the brewery is independently owned – was not even mentioned by Cottone. The simplification, the erosion, of his definition tells a revealing story about how craft beer has developed over the last 30-odd years, and provides a neat summary of the problems and paradoxes that come with any attempt to define craft beer – or craft breweries.

---

[18]"What Qualifies As Craft Beer?" *USA Today,* 13th January 2013: https://eu.usatoday.com/story/money/business/2013/01/13/what-qualifies-as-craft-beer-depends-on-whom-you-ask/1566338/

The problem with defining craft beer as coming from "a small brewery"

Vince Cottone set out to replace descriptions of a brewing scene that was based on the size of the brewer – and then included the size of the brewer as the first criterion in his new definition. Effectively, he kept hold of the problems he was trying to solve, and added various other issues under a banner I'm sure he thought would never come in for as much scrutiny as it subsequently did.

He undoubtedly did so because he believed craft brewers *were* small brewers; he just didn't think that was the only thing we should be thinking about them. Small doesn't necessarily mean good, and he was trying to define brewers he thought were better than the mainstream. But by keeping "small" in there, he gave craft beer what would turn out to be its biggest definitional headache.

The early pioneers of craft brewing were not looking to get rich. Many of them left comfortable, well-paid professions to do something they assumed would make them far less money but give them a more fulfilled life. But some of them did get very rich indeed, because it turned out that there were a lot more people who were interested in drinking flavourful, complex beer than they could ever have imagined.

The first, and most obvious, thing about size is that it's relative: what's small in the US might be huge in UK terms. This is why the BA's long-held definition of craft beer, which we'll look at in some detail shortly, was not fit for purpose in any other country. To be fair, it never claimed to be – the BA had no interest and no obligation to define craft brewing outside its own geographical remit. But the modern craft beer movement started in America and looks to America for guidance, so we end up with people attempting to use a definition that is hopelessly unfit for purpose where they are.

More importantly, irrespective of what country you're in, and how big is big and how small is small, I'm sure that back in 1986, no one involved in the young American craft beer scene could have imagined that, by 2018, craft beer globally would be worth almost $38bn.[19] Craft beer is now routinely credited by analysts with driving growth in the beer market overall. Many leading craft breweries operate at a size and scale and with a level of technological sophistication that is indistinguishable from the smaller end of the "industrial" breweries they supposedly stand against. In the US, Yuengling, the biggest company that meets the BA's definition of a craft brewery, is the sixth or seventh largest brewery in the country overall, just behind Diageo, which owns Guinness.[20] The Boston Beer Company is ninth biggest overall, Sierra Nevada tenth and New Belgium eleventh, all ahead of a company called the Craft Brew Alliance which, according to the BA, is not a craft brewery at all because it is owned by Anheuser-Busch InBev.

Here's one of the great paradoxes of craft beer: the idea of buying from a small brewery is inherently appealing to a certain group of people. If that group of people grows big enough, then craft as an industry cannot stay small. That's fine, you might argue – it just means there's room for more breweries. Rather than three massive ones, we can have 5,000 tiny ones. That would work perfectly if small was the *only* appeal that craft beer had. But size exists within a bunch of different motivations.

For example, I live two miles away from the Beavertown Brewery in North London. Beavertown is local to me and I

---

[19] https://www.globenewswire.com/news-release/2019/01/25/1705363/0/en/Global-Craft-Beer-Market-Will-Reach-USD-92-230-Million-By-2025-Zion-Market-Research.html
[20] https://www.brewersassociation.org/press-releases/brewers-association-announces-top-50-brewing-companies-by-sales-volume-of-2019/

drank Beavertown beers when they were being brewed in the basement of a restaurant just down the road. But they grew because the hype around them meant people across around the country wanted their beers too. Five years ago, if I visited, say, Sheffield or Bristol, specifically in search of local beers, I would often find bars that sold Beavertown beers and be urged to try them: "Hey, we finally managed to get some Beavertown! They're so much better than the local guys!"

The conditions that created the craft beer boom in the UK – the constant, "always-on" conversation of social media, the close networks and collaborations between brewers, bloggers and retailers – also made it very easy for craft to scale quickly. After Beavertown sold a stake to Heineken in 2018 and gained access to the giant's distribution networks, its sales increased by 500 per cent in the first twelve months.[21] Some of this growth came from Heineken's aggressive sales tactics and their routes into major supermarket chains. But in a mature, declining beer market, you don't get double- let alone triple-digit growth unless there's huge pent-up demand. Is a craft brewer that started off small supposed to ignore that demand? When millions of people say they want to try their beer, should popular craft brewers simply tell them to go away?

Some craft drinkers would argue yes, they should. Look at the conversation around BrewDog. Founded in 2007, by 2019, BrewDog had broken into the world's top twenty beer brands (measured in terms of value) reaching number 19[22], one place above Carlsberg, making it the largest UK-based beer brand.[23] To many craft beer fans, BrewDog

[21] https://www.thegrocer.co.uk/results/beavertown-off-trade-sales-surge-500-after-heineken-sale/593861.article
[22] https://brandfinance.com/knowledge-centre/reports/brand-finance-beers-25-2019/
[23] Guinness, which comes in at number 10, is technically a UK-owned brand because Diageo is a British company. But Guinness is based in Ireland and is seen emphatically as an Irish brand.

ceased to be a bona fide craft brewery long before this point. It was simply too big and too popular to be considered craft. In 2017 BrewDog sold a 22 per cent stake to a private equity firm, leading some former fans to accuse it of selling out. But this stake keeps it well within the ownership terms laid down by the BA. This doesn't matter to beer geeks on social media: to some, BrewDog is now "too big to be independent" – a logical fallacy that illustrates perfectly the tensions within discussions of craft beer.

It may sound like nonsense when subjected to rational analysis, but it's an argument that, as a music fan, I am intimately familiar with. As a teenager, I was passionately into "indie" or "alternative" music, and it's a comparison that will be keeping us company throughout this book. Every alternative music fan has a band they adored, and part of the pleasure was the sense of discovery, the fact that you were into this band when few people were. They weren't getting wall-to-wall play on commercial radio. Maybe you even had to order their records in or visit specialist shops to get them. Your mates hadn't heard of them. And this all meant your love for them was purer, more authentic, than the sheeple who just bought whatever was on A-list rotation. And then The Clash/U2/Depeche Mode/Nirvana/Oasis/Coldplay/Arctic Monkeys/Mumford & Sons (delete according to age) became successful and started playing stadium gigs, at which point we former fans would accuse them of "selling out", insisting that we were into them before they were cool, and emphatically declaring that we preferred their earlier stuff. As with some craft beer fans, we were part of a scene. It was cool and we used it partially to define ourselves against the mainstream. When the mainstream started liking it too, we blamed the band for being too successful. (Apart from Coldplay of course, who were always awful.)

In the United States, Boston Brewing has suffered a similar fate to BrewDog. Discerning craft beer geeks now wouldn't be seen dead near the brand. They insist the beers have changed, that they've been blanded out and dumbed down. And yet, breathing down Boston's neck, Sierra Nevada is also worth in excess of $1 billion. Founder Ken Grossman is a billionaire.[24] When asked about the size of his brewery recently, he made no apologies for it. "It's a grow or die mentality," he said. "If our brand isn't growing, somebody else's will".[25] Spoken like a true capitalist. Yet while I'm sure there are people who would argue that Sierra Nevada is no longer a proper craft brewery, it's not an argument I have ever heard myself. Grossman has somehow managed to maintain indie credibility whilst becoming incredibly rich. Partly that's because Sierra Nevada's beers remain consistently among the best in the world, and partly it's because he's a great guy who embodies everything we want a craft brewer to be. But there's more to it than that.

Anyone with younger siblings will have gone through a version of what BrewDog's James Watt or Boston's Jim Koch have experienced. The oldest child is the first to rebel, the first to have to argue to stay up late, to go out on their own, to have sleepovers. They fight all the battles, and then a year or two later, the younger sibling seems to get the same benefits without having to fight any of the battles. In the UK, BrewDog was the first craft brewer to grow to such a size. And in the US, it was Boston. In being the first craft brewer to achieve industrial scale, Boston suffered publicly as their success caused significant problems for a size-based definition of craft beer. When the BA first created its own definition, "small" meant an output no greater than two million barrels per year. This figure was chosen because it was the cut-off for the small brewers' tax differential introduced in 1976. In 2010, when Boston was rapidly approaching that two-million barrier, the BA simply raised it to six million. Both Boston and the BA received a great deal of online scorn for what was widely seen as a cynical move.

---

[24] https://www.bloomberg.com/news/articles/2015-01-20/sierra-nevada-founder-grossman-becomes-billionaire-on-pale-ales
[25] https://www.forbes.com/profile/ken-grossman/

Should any other brewer pass the same threshold (Sierra Nevada is currently somewhere around 1.2 million barrels so it probably won't happen any time soon) they're unlikely to receive a fraction of the same scrutiny.

To be fair to the BA, from an industry point of view, leaving the definition at two million barrels and declaring Boston to be no longer a craft brewer could have caused catastrophic harm to the craft beer scene as a whole.

Imagine the BA had stuck to its initial limit. Looking at the market data, Boston's two million barrels would have had to be subtracted from the total amount of craft beer being brewed and added to the total of big macro beer. Twelve months later, this would then show up in the data as a sharp fall in craft beer volume and market share. We live in an age when journalism is hurried and attention spans are short. Many journalists – and a surprising number of beer bloggers – are desperate to write the "craft beer bubble bursts" headline and be the first to report the demise of such a powerful movement. This artificial adjustment to market data, based on a technicality of definition, would allow such a story to spread. If it did so, it could easily lead to craft beers being dropped by bars, shops and wholesalers who believed the demand for craft was waning – all as a direct result of the demand for craft actually *increasing*. This is why a definition based on size is paradoxical and, ultimately, potentially harmful for the craft beer sector.

Also, smallness isn't necessarily a virtue. I've tasted many bland – and some downright unpleasant – beers from major corporations, but by far the worst beers I've ever tasted are from small craft breweries who knowingly put out a beer that has faults, because they believe they can't afford to pour it away. Some of them simply aren't very good at brewing to begin with, or even aware that their beer sucks. I've judged in home brewing competitions where the average quality of the beer is higher than that in competitions featuring small commercial breweries. The

58

home brewer obsesses over every batch, and if it's not good enough, they don't enter it into the competition – there are many no-shows on the day. Many small craft brewers would do the same, but not all. So size is no guarantee of quality, and in their willingness to compromise, some small brewers – and I'll name one name later on – can be as guilty of bastardising our ideas about what craft beer is as big corporations are.

The problem with defining craft brewing as "using traditional methods and ingredients"

Define "craft beer" with reference to "traditional methods and ingredients," and you then have to define what that means too. Defining "small" led to all sorts of headaches. Defining "traditional methods and ingredients" replaces one thorny definitional problem with another, allows words to be twisted from their original meaning and intent, and allows measures intended to protect an industry to be turned into an attack on it.

If you're a fan of craft beer, it's hard to disagree that the methods and ingredients used to make the beer are pretty important. Big commercial brewers use all sorts of cheaper adjuncts to bulk out expensive malting barley. Stella Artois is now brewed with maize. Budweiser owner Anheuser Busch is the biggest purchaser of rice in the United States. In many countries, the very cheapest beers are brewed with corn syrup or sucrose. These beers suffer a significant compromise in their character: malted barley is at least as much a contributor of flavour to beer as it is a source of fermentable sugars.

The use of cheap adjuncts in beer is as old as brewing itself. Until relatively recently, these could be poisonous, even fatal. Today, a commercially available beer brewed with cheap adjuncts is highly unlikely to kill you or even make you ill, but it still leads to great, classic beer styles being bastardised or even threatened with extinction. Think about the character of a true Czech pilsner. Pilsner Urquell – the original that all others supposedly followed – remains a stone-cold classic (even if it could never be considered craft because of who now owns it, and also because it's almost 180 years old, but let's not go there again). Compare this to industrially produced "pilsner" beers rushed through factories around the world, and the argument that craft should at least in part be about the preservation of traditional production methods and ingredients seems inarguable.

A few years ago, I was lucky enough to have lunch at Seattle's Pike Place brewpub with the brewery's founder, Charles Finkel, and his wife Rose Ann. "What do you fancy to drink?" asked Charles, sliding the day's tap list over to me.

My passion for beer is like a flame. Sometimes it burns brightly, other times it flickers low, and every now and then, the snark of beer Twitter, the cynicism of some commercial practices, or even simple palate fatigue can threaten to extinguish it altogether. I remember that moment in Seattle in 2016 so vividly because the flame blazed up as if someone had thrown overly-laboured metaphorical paraffin on it. I just checked the tap list online, and it hasn't changed much. As you'd expect, there are a variety of IPAs. But there's also a German-style Helles, a British-style golden ale, a Czech-style Pilsner, a Scottish-style Wee Heavy, a strong stout and a Belgian-style Tripel, all from the same brewery, all conforming to tight style guidelines. It's a beer list I could never get bored of, even if it feels curiously old-fashioned in today's craft beer scene. And it exists thanks to a dedication to preserving and exploring traditional methods and ingredients.

The problem is, as anyone familiar with the German *Reinheitsgebot* and its effects on the German beer scene can warn you, there's a danger in *mandating* traditional

60

ingredients and processes rather than simply *supporting* them and campaigning for their continued existence. This (allegedly) centuries-old purity law states that beer can only be made from hops, barley, yeast, water, and sometimes wheat. While it does have its passionate supporters, most German craft brewers and pundits loathe it, blaming it for stifling innovation in German brewing and holding it back as the rest of the world races ahead.[26]

If traditional methods and ingredients were still part of an official definition of craft beer, then craft beer would be very limited in its scope for innovation. We could kiss goodbye to New England IPAs made hazy with the addition of oat or wheat flour. No more hibiscus goses, no fruited kettle sours, no pastry stouts. These would all break the rules and fall short of the definition of craft beer. And that would suffocate craft beer, as well as annoying the hell out of many who brew and drink it.

The problem with defining craft beer as "hand-crafted"

In the early days of the modern craft beer movement, "hand-crafted" was one of the strongest aspects of its appeal. A year after Cottone's definition was published, Charlie Papazian – seen by many as the godfather-cum-midwife of the American craft beer movement – offered his own neat, elegant definition of a craft brewery, as "Any brewery using the manual arts and skills of a brewer to create its products".[27]

"Hand-crafted" and "hand-made" are beautiful, reassuring

---

[26] I visited Munich, where the Reinheitsgebot was first applied, in 2016, the 500-year anniversary of the law being passed in Bavaria. For a full discussion of its impact and pros and cons, check out the final section of my book *Miracle Brew: Adventures in the Nature of Beer* (Unbound, London, 2017).

[27] *The New Brewer*, Spring 1987

terms. They differentiate craft from industry in the cleanest and most vivid way possible. And of all the definitional aspects of craft beer, this is the one that chimes most closely with the broader concept of what a "craft" is. But in a process as complex as brewing, what does "hand-crafted" actually mean?

In his book *Cræft* (2017), Alexander Langlands believes human effort, the expending of energy and the movement of the body, is an essential part of what makes something "craft" or not, and explores the complicated relationship between craft and the use of tools with reference to hedge-trimming and topiary. Hedges have been planted and maintained since agriculture began. In the first century CE, Pliny the Younger described box hedges in Tuscany that had been trimmed to resemble various animals. The Romans would have used a sickle or hedging hook. Over time, technologies such as opposing blades joined by a screw, like scissors and garden shears, were developed to make the job easier, but all still involved the person using them to manipulate their body and supply physical power to do so. As tools become more sophisticated and turn into machines, human involvement becomes less important, until you get to an electric hedge trimmer that gets its power from a plug socket. Langlands argues that, at this point, topiary has stopped being a "craft" in a truly honest sense.[28]

I've watched hand-crafted beer being made many times, and occasionally contributed a tokenistic amount of my own labour for the sake of appearance. I've carefully tipped sacks of malted barley into a mash tun, then mixed it with water using a wooden paddle to get a smooth, uniform consistency. As the mash tun gets fuller, it gets harder to move the paddle through the thick, porridge-like mash, and you're trying to do so at an awkward angle, leaning in yet at the same time holding your arms high. They soon begin to

---

[28]Langlands, Alexander, *Cræft: How Traditional Crafts Are About More than Just Making*, (Faber & Faber, London, 2017) p.36.

ache, and towards the end there's some serious exertion required.

Once the grain is mashed, the wort is drained off. To ensure there's as much sugary extract from the grain as possible, a metal arm is attached to the top of the mash tun that circulates and sprays the grain with water, a process known as sparging. When that's finished, the wet grain, now far heavier than when it was emptied into the tun, has to be dug out manually, with a shovel, into bags that have to be carried or dragged out of the brewery.

This is as hand-made as beer gets. Almost. Most breweries have mechanised arms inside the mash tun to take away that arduous labour. But if we wanted to be brutally strict about it, we could argue that even in the brewery that mashes in by hand, the sparging arm, which is motorised, means this particular beer is not entirely hand-made. Why isn't the brewer doing it by hand, with a watering can, instead?

Any modern brewer would instantly tell you that the sparging arm is a simple piece of technology that does the job far more accurately and efficiently than any human with a watering can or hose could. Isn't the sparging arm just an adaptation of a hose or watering can? The difference is that the sparging arm is motorised and requires no human effort – it's less *craeft*, like the electric hedge cutter. But is this a reasonable place to draw the line between what is craft and what is not? More manual labour at this point wouldn't result in better beer, and would just mean that the brewer has to stand there for an hour rinsing grain by hand when they could be doing something else to improve the quality or appeal of their beer. There's not a huge amount of knowledge-based skill being lost by replacing a brewer wielding a hose with a mechanical arm powered by a small motor. Also, there's still so much physical action in the rest of the brewing process that, unlike Langlands's hedge clippers, where the electric motor is replacing most of the effort of human labour, the use of a sparging arm makes minimal difference to the overall calories being burned during a brew day. So maybe we allow that. But then where do we draw the line? Where does beer stop being truly hand-made?

We could argue that it's at the point where the tool becomes a machine, when it removes the need for manipulative skill, bodily controlled movements, the point when, according to Langlands, "the tool mutes their level of engagement with the material properties of the entity they are working".[29]

But as soon as craft breweries began to grow, they started using tools and machines that made it easier to brew at scale, to be more precise in what they were trying to achieve, and to save time on back-breaking menial tasks to spend more time on designing great beer. Getting a mash tun that automatically cleans itself instead of the brewer having to get inside and scrub it certainly mutes the level of engagement with the material properties of the malt, and most brewers would wholeheartedly say that's a good thing. Would we say a gourmet chef is less gourmet if they use a dishwasher rather than washing up themselves?

That's why the craft beer world forgot about "hand-crafted" pretty quickly. But in doing so, it began its drift away from what "craft" actually means. Ask anyone outside brewing what separates craft from industrial production, and "hand-made" or "hand-crafted" will appear in the top answers. When "craft" stops meaning "hand-made," it starts to mean something else.

---

[29]Ibid.

The problem with defining craft beer as "uncompromised"

What is "compromise"? The *Oxford English Dictionary* (OED) offers two separate definitions.

The first of these is "the expedient acceptance of standards that are lower than is desirable."

If this is what we mean by the word, then it's fair that anyone who drinks craft beer is highly likely to expect it to be uncompromised. It works in a similar way to "traditional methods and ingredients" in that it supports the preservation of quality and style. The most common fear drinkers have when a global brewing corporation swallows up a beloved craft brewer is that the accountants will insist upon cost-cutting measures that will have a detrimental effect on the quality of the beer.

Big brewers are part of an economic system that *necessitates* compromise in this sense. Any large corporation is legally obliged to place the maximisation of shareholder wealth above any other commercial consideration. A company's fortunes are based on the expectation that shareholder dividends will perpetually increase. But infinite growth is impossible. So when sales growth doesn't fuel the bottom line, companies invariably move to cost-cutting measures to improve the numbers instead. It's short-sighted, it's wrong, but everyone does it, because if they don't, the company management will lose their jobs or the shares will plummet in value, allowing the company to potentially be swallowed up by a rival.

Compromise is also driven by retailers, particularly supermarkets. In return for wide-scale distribution, supermarkets demand the keenest price possible from their suppliers. Each time the deal is renegotiated on a successful product, supermarkets are likely to want a greater quantity at a progressively lower unit cost. Eventually, producers are faced with a dilemma: they're now so reliant on the supermarket's custom that they can't afford to give up the contract. But the only way to make the product for the price the supermarket is willing to pay is to compromise on product quality. This is why mainstream standard lagers suck, and why they have no option but to suck because the brewer is sometimes making as little as 1p per can profit on a sale to a big chain. It's why the tinned "food" you grew up eating no longer tastes as good as it did, and it's why big-brand cider contains as little as 35 per cent apple juice.

And why do the nasty supermarkets do this? Because evil bastards like you and me expect them to sell a ridiculously wide range of products at unfeasibly low prices. We're all in on this.

Craft beer has succeeded in circumventing the inevitability of this kind of compromise by largely operating outside the mainstream economic system. Craft beer has its own distribution system of taprooms, independent craft beer bars and bottle shops. Craft breweries that are independently owned are answerable only to themselves, not the doctrine of maximising shareholder value.

Remember though, that the *OED* offers two definitions of compromise. The second is "an agreement or settlement of a dispute that is reached by each side making concessions". Compromise in this sense is usually seen as a positive thing – irreconcilable positions being moderated to a point that everyone can work with.

But both definitions involved climbing down from standards or positions that were previously seen as immovable. This means, the choice between the two interpretations of "compromise" can be subjective.

For example, if we're talking about compromising a product, session IPA is a total compromise. IPA is a highly

66

hopped, high-ABV beer style. Its fans want to drink more of it, without necessarily getting hammered. So a low-strength IPA is a compromise that, depending on your point of view, is either the brewer and drinker making concessions to each other in order that one can sell more beer to the other, or the bastardisation and literal watering down of a classic beer style. Either way, it's compromised, and therefore, under Cottone's definition, not a legitimate craft beer style.

The broader economic question of compromise for a craft brewing business is more complex. Do we strike off a craft brewer for the sin of selling beer through a supermarket, chain retailer or large pub group? Whether or not you think so, this discussion of compromise illustrates why it hasn't survived as part of any attempt at a definition of craft beer.

The problem with defining craft beer as "marketed locally"

Again, this final aspect of Cottone's definition speaks of a time when craft brewers were exclusively serving local markets, so it made sense to celebrate it in opposition to the creeping homogeneity of corporate capitalism. If anything, the importance and appeal of locally sourced food and drink has only grown since Cottone wrote his book. In an age of food miles, a yearning for authenticity and a desire to keep money circulating within local economies rather than going to the shareholders of faceless, remote corporations, supporting local producers hasn't been so popular since it was the only choice we had. In the United States, the craft beer scene is moving hyper-local, with the vast majority of new craft brewery openings being taprooms or brewpubs. "Marketed locally" is certainly a vital part of what craft beer is and why it appeals as we enter the third decade of the 21st century.

The problem is, if you make it part of the *definition* of craft beer, you're stipulating that it can *only* be local.

This means that any craft brewery with international or even national distribution is no longer a craft brewery. So we say goodbye not only to the giants like Sierra Nevada, BrewDog and Brooklyn, but also to any beer you can readily get hold of in your local craft beer bar or bottle shop if it was brewed more than a couple of hours' drive away. If you wanted to be really firm about your definition of "marketed locally", you could rule out any brewery that makes effective use of its social media accounts or website, or offers its beers for sale from an online shop.

"Marketed locally" also throws up the absurd notion whereby a beer is craft or not depending on where you got hold of it. That can of Cloudwater DIPA is craft as hell if you bought it from Beer Moth in Manchester's Northern Quarter. It's no more craft than Heineken if you bought it at a Meet the Brewer event at Cloudwater's tap room in Bermondsey.

Sorry, Vince

Given that no one I am aware of is even trying to argue that Vince Cottone's definition of a craft brewer should still be in common use, it may seem unfair to the point of viciousness to spend so long tearing it apart, element by element. I've done so not to have a go at Cottone or his work, which I admire. His definition incorporates all the issues that have been key talking points around craft beer over the last three decades, and therefore provides us with a useful framework to discuss those issues. Most people who love craft beer would invariably prefer to support a brewer who is small-scale, respects traditional methods and ingredients, still does things by hand, doesn't compromise, and has a local focus, so these are all useful concepts. The problem arises when you state that these ideas *define* a craft brewery rather than simply *describe* what craft breweries are usually or often like. Elephants are almost always grey. But if we were to therefore say that the colour grey is part of the definition of an elephant, then a white elephant is no longer an elephant. The more separate points there are to a definition, the harder it becomes to comply with that definition. So if a brewer grows, or gets a machine, or ships beer abroad, they're no longer a craft brewer.

By working through Cottone's definition in this way, I'm proposing that *any* attempt to create a strict definition for the purpose of distinguishing between what is craft and what is not – which is the primary function of a strict definition – is unworkable.

Which is why it would take the industry bodies formed by craft brewers another twenty years from Cottone's attempt before they had another go at doing it.

The problems with the American Brewers' Association definition of craft beer

In the early 2000s, craft beer had grown to a size and scale that had not only outgrown Vince Cottone's definition, but had also started to be noticed by big brewers who were getting pissed off with how popular it was at beer industry wholesaler conferences. The Board of the newly formed Brewers' Association came together and voted to define an American craft brewer as one that was small, independent and traditional. They also went to painstaking efforts to define exactly what each of these words meant:

> **Small:** Annual production of beer less than two million barrels. Beer production is attributed to a brewer according to the rules of alternating proprietorships. FMBs [Flavoured Malt Beverages] are not considered beer for purposes of this definition.
> **Independent:** Less than 25% of the craft brewery is owned or controlled (or equivalent economic interest) by an alcoholic beverage industry member who is not themselves a craft brewer.
> **Traditional:** A brewer who has either an all-malt flagship (the beer which represents the greatest volume among that brewer's

brands) or has at least 50% of its volume in either all-malt beers or in beers which use adjuncts to enhance rather than lighten flavor.[30]

At first glance this is much more useful as a measurable, implementable definition, both more streamlined and more practical than Cottone's version. Even more than Cottone, it's zeroing in on the nature of the brewer rather than the nature of the beer, but not exclusively so.

One intriguing aspect of Cottone's definition is that it made no mention whatsoever of who owns the brewery. Maybe if he was writing a few years later, he would have included this, but it's safe to say that if he assumed craft brewing would remain small in scale, then issues around corporate ownership would never arise. In the early 1980s, ownership probably seemed about as relevant to a definition of a craft brewery as the shape of the fermenters or the square footage of the brewhouse.

By 2005, it was an issue.

As Big Beer shifted into gear on its denigrate, regulate and replicate strategy, no one could blame an association of small brewers from trying to resist such cynical and unfair behaviour. The BA is a trade association. Like any trade association, it exists to protect the interests of its members and promote their businesses. As it says on its website, the BA is "The Organization of Brewers, for Brewers and by Brewers".[31] Their definition of a craft brewer – not craft beer, remember – is no more and no less than a description of the type of brewers that are eligible for membership of its club, and it is whatever they would like it to be: like any club, it has the right to decide whom it allows in.

---

[30]Quoted in Acitelli, Tom, *The Audacity of Hops: The History of America's Craft Beer Revolution*, (Chicago Review Press, Chicago, 2013) p.314.
[31]https://www.brewersassociation.org/who-we-are/

One of the biggest problems in navigating the definition of craft beer starts when the membership criteria for that club become confused with an attempt to create an overriding, universally applicable definition of what craft beer is – a mistake made by beer drinkers worldwide who are searching for such a definition, and also by both supporters and critics of the BA and its agenda.

When we talk about the definition of craft beer, we're talking at cross-purposes. The membership criteria for an American trade association cannot work as a globally applicable, platonic ideal of craft beer. The weight of expectation and responsibility is too much for any such definition to bear, and it wasn't long before the BA's version started running into problems.

We've already discussed the issue with the "small brewery" clause. When small means anything up to six million barrels, it includes a good chunk of the top ten largest brewers in the USA, one of the biggest beer markets by volume in the world, and is therefore effectively meaningless in any broader sense, despite the best of intentions.

The next headache arose a few years later with increasing concerns over the third clause mandating the need for "traditional" all-malt beers. As we've already discussed, craft beer rapidly became anything but traditional. So in 2014, the clause about ingredients was amended to apply to a brewery that has a "majority of its total beverage alcohol volume in beers whose flavor derives from *traditional or innovative* brewing ingredients in their fermentation". (My italics.) So in other words, the ingredients in your beer no longer made any real difference to whether you were a craft brewer or not.

This had the immediate effect of making Yuengling the new biggest "craft brewer" in the country, and therefore, the world. America's oldest brewery, the sixth-biggest in the country, which was turning out lagers brewed with cheap corn and rice adjuncts that were not so different from those brewed by Budweiser, was now a craft brewer on the grounds that it was still independently owned – the last remaining meaningful plank in the BA's definition.

The tensions inherent in "traditional or innovative ingredients" were apparent, and in 2018, this "outdated" element of the definition of a craft brewer was dispensed with altogether. At the time of writing, the BA's definition of a craft brewer reads:

Small
Annual production of 6 million barrels of beer or less (approximately 3% of U.S. annual sales). Beer production is attributed to a brewer according to rules of alternating proprietorships.
Independent
Less than 25% of the craft brewery is owned or controlled (or equivalent economic interest) by a beverage alcohol industry member that is not itself a craft brewer.
Brewer
(i) Has a TTB Brewer's Notice and (ii) makes beer.[32]

Now, the type, style, ingredients and quality of beer you make are all irrelevant. All you need to be a craft brewer is to be small in scale (when small no longer means small), to not be owned by a big corporation (unless that big corporation owns itself) and to be in possession of a brewers' licence (no shit).

As always, there was sound reasoning behind a change that looks ridiculous to anyone who forgets that this is not a definition of craft beer, but criteria for the membership of a trade association. Many of the BA's members are branching out to make cider, kombucha, mead and, gods forgive them, hard seltzers. Boston Brewing's cider division, headed by its Angry Orchard brand, and its Truly hard selzer product, are now bigger than the core beer business, and we've already

[32]https://www.brewersassociation.org/statistics-and-data/craft-brewer-definition/

been through why the BA can't let Boston slip out of its definition of craft brewing. So long as a producer of fizzy fermented drinks still brews at least one beer, even if it's an inferior copy of Bud, it's still a craft brewer.

From the point of view of a trade association, we're now in a useful place. The definition is so simple, clear, measurable and precise, there can be no confusion about what is and is not a craft brewer. There's absolutely no way that big corporate brewers can pretend, obfuscate, or replicate.

The problem is, we've also reached a position where the word "craft" is not just arguable, but completely irrelevant to what we're now describing. If Yuengling Light – a mass-produced, industrial, tasteless, low-calorie beer brewed with corn syrup – is a craft beer, and Goose Island Bourbon Country Stout – which scores a maximum 100 in its class on beer rating websites Beer Advocate and RateBeer, and is named ninth-best Imperial Stout in the world by the former and fourth-best by the latter – is *not* a craft beer, on the grounds that Goose Island is now owned by A-B InBev, then we've lost sight of any sensible concept of what "craft beer" might be, and started talking about something else entirely. Whatever that is, we shouldn't be calling it craft beer.

Which is precisely why the BA, along with other, similar trade associations around the world, is pulling back from doing so.

In June 2017, the BA launched a new logo – which they referred to as an "independent seal" – and urged their members to use it on all their packaging and promotional material, arguing, quite reasonably, that drinkers had a right to know who had brewed their beer.

A month later, the UK's Society of Independent Brewers (SIBA) launched their own version, citing confusion in the market following high-profile buyouts of brewers such as Camden Town by the corporate giants that craft brewers had initially stood against.

That same year, the Australian Craft Beer Industry Association changed its name to the Independent Brewers Association (IBA). In 2019, it duly introduced its own seal, with a massive promotional campaign called Indie Beer Day, to urge its members to use it, and beer drinkers to look for it. Similar seals have now launched around the world.

The word "craft" is hanging on in there in some places, but the trend is clear: what we used to call craft beer no longer wants to be known by that term. Independence – which didn't even feature in Vince Cottone's original definition, remember – is now the only aspect that is deemed to matter. Via a series of tactical retreats forced by the advance of Big Beer into craft territory, the battle for the term "craft beer" is lost; the corporates have seemingly triumphed with their strategy of denigrate, regulate and replicate yet again.

Despite this, I want to argue that it is worth keeping the word "craft" and that it can and should be applied both to beers that are brewed by small, independent brewers and, where appropriate, to beers that are not.

But before I do, it's worth reiterating why it's important that the global brewing industry has a clearly defined, strong independent sector, whatever we call it, even if it's now evolved into something that can no longer usefully be described as craft. If my dismantling of various definitions of craft beer sounds like a criticism of the motives or intentions of the BA or any other body involved in promoting or protecting small brewers, it shouldn't. As I explained in the last chapter, small, independent brewers are absolutely vital in driving the success not just of craft beer, but of the wider beer industry, and fans of interesting, flavourful beer have a basic right as consumers to know where their beer is from and who made it.

But we also have to consider that the craft/independent beer movement didn't get as big as it is now *just* because of a preference to support small, independent businesses. Craft is now hitting the mainstream drinker. If it wants to grow further – and there's no reason why any craft brewer should not want to – they need to engage with people who are not that bothered about ownership, or people who think supporting a small, independent business is a nice-to-have, but not essential, factor in their choice of beer. If someone is perfectly happy drinking Bud, or even Goose Island IPA, knowing that these brands are owned by a big corporation, how is telling them that Burning Sky or Farnum Hill is independently-owned going to make any difference to their purchase intentions?

In my marketing days, we used to talk about the difference between features and benefits. The pithiest explanation I've ever heard of it is that no one really wants to buy a three-quarter-inch drill-bit; what they want to buy is the best possible means of making a three-quarter-inch hole. The word "craft" is evocative; it suggests not just the physical benefit of tastier beer, but also the emotional benefits of tapping into concepts of authenticity, provenance and experience that people currently care about in a much broader context than just beer. Independence is a *feature*, a characteristic, of the brewers who make craft beer. The *benefit* of a brewer's independent status – if independence is the main thing we're now talking about – is not immediately clear to the Bud drinker who might be thinking of switching.

The benefits to the consumer of buying beer from an independent brewer need to be clearly articulated and explained, in a way they didn't need to be when we were just talking about craft beer and small brewers were the only companies making it. A seal of assurance is all well and good – but it's only the very start of telling that story.

Defining and protecting the small, independent brewing sector is a cause I believe in and will defend in any way I can. I just believe that this is now an entirely different thing from "craft beer", and that "craft beer" ultimately turns out to have always been the wrong banner to rally behind for this purpose. Sure, there's a significant overlap, but ultimately we shouldn't be relying on the membership criteria of trade organisations around the world for a close definition of a concept such as craft beer, whose appeal lies not just in quality, but in emotional resonances, beliefs, and a philosophy about how things should be done.

There is an alternative definition of craft beer lurking in the shadows that gets much closer to these ideas, but I'm going to predict with some confidence that this will be the first time you've ever seen it.

The definitional problem with trying to define craft beer on its own terms

In an article for the sixth edition of the *Good Beer Guide Belgium* (2009)[33], beer importer and writer Dan Shelton – who imports Belgian beers into the United States – offered a set of criteria that to his mind "separate the commercial places from the craft places":

1. *Ingredients*: Does the brewer seek the best possible ingredients or is s/he more concerned about keeping costs down?
2. *Methods and equipment*: The brewery's intent – does the brewery do everything it can to maintain quality or does it let things slip as it grows? Is the brewery making the best beer it can?
3. *The brewer's spirit*: Does the beer reflect the brewer's personality or is it simply generic and lacking in faults? Are they just following the market, or trying to do something special?
4. *Company structure*: Who's calling the shots? It's not necessarily about company size, but does the brewer decide what beers

---

[33]Shelton, Dan, "Spotting a craft brewer", in Webb, Tim, *Good Beer Guide Belgium*, (6th edition, CAMRA, St Albans, 2009) p.13.

are brewed, or does the marketing department?

5. *Control*: Is the brewer able to exercise some control over how the beer turns out or is s/he simply throwing in ingredients and hoping for the best?

Shelton refers to this list as a "work in progress". It's flexible enough to allow a non-craft brewer to brew a craft beer, should they want to. As Shelton comments, "It says nothing about the size of the brewer. It just happens that the larger breweries are the ones that are more likely to break these rules." It's also flexible enough that brewers won't get caught on the barbed wire of growing too big, or putting something weird into the kettle, or selling a stake to someone else – all that matters is that they keep putting the beer first, and making the best beer they can.

But despite being published in 2009, I haven't seen this definition discussed or reproduced anywhere other than in a book that's long been out of print, superseded by newer editions. A Google search for "Dan Shelton craft beer" returns just two blog posts discussing it, and one of these is my own from 2013.

I think there are a few reasons for this. The first is that it's not easy to remember. It's not simple. Every time I want to refer to it, I have to go back and check what these specific five points are.

Second, it doesn't serve the purposes of craft brewing industry bodies at all. It doesn't work if you want to exclude a great craft brewer who sells their business to a big corporation. This was kind of Shelton's whole point – it resolves the Yuengling Light/Goose Island Bourbon County problem. But that means it's been ignored by the most influential industry bodies on the craft beer scene.

Finally – and most importantly – if you're looking for measurable criteria which you can use to run the rule over a brewery and state conclusively whether it is craft or not,

Shelton's definition is utterly useless. How can you accurately discern whether a brewer is truly looking for the best possible ingredients, or seeking to cut costs, unless you actually work for the brewery? Even if you know the brewer well, what criteria are you going to use to decide whether this beer reflects their spirit or personality as much as the last one did? And how do you know if the brewer is in full control of the process or just hoping for the best, unless you're inside their head? To a great many people – not just industry trade associations – a definition that cannot be measured and used for evaluation is no definition at all.

If you don't want "craft beer" any more, can we have it back?

In this chapter, we've followed the story of brave attempts to define "craft beer" being whittled down and eroded, until they were not talking about "craft" in any direct sense at all.

Comparing membership criteria for the craft beer club with an honest definition that seeks to define craft brewing on its own terms, we can see that we're faced with a choice between potential definitions that are either measurable but irrelevant or impractical, or relevant but unmeasurable and impractical. Even when we try to put emotion aside and work through each idea and criterion logically, we meet with obstacles at every turn.

So why keep going on about it? Why not simply declare, as so many people who drink it already have, that "craft beer" is a debased, meaningless concept?

The short answer to that question brings us back to the 276 definitions of terrorism: just because you fail to define a concept does not mean that that concept has no meaning or does not exist. The sun still shone when people believed it was a horse-drawn chariot arcing across the sky.

79

While a precise, measurable, technical definition may be impossible to agree upon, I still believe it is important to pin down a common understanding of what craft beer means in a looser, broader sense.

Even before we taste the stuff, the abstract idea of "craft beer" has an innate appeal to millions of people around the world. Attempts to define that idea have led us down a cul-de-sac that is quite removed from what that abstract idea might be. That's why I thought it might be worth reversing out of that cul-de-sac, scrapping any existing attempt at defining what craft beer might be, and starting again. Instead of attrition to the point where all that matters is ownership, let's start by putting the question of ownership to one side and exploring instead ideas of craft that can be used to evaluate any brewery of any size or scale.

We could do a lot worse than using Dan Shelton's definition as a starting point. But even though that definition has appeared this early in the book, the truth is I'd forgotten about it until quite late in this project. Looking at it now, further exploration of it would keep us pinned firmly to the world of brewing, and I'd already decided to start off on a different path that takes us on a more scenic route. So for now, let's forget about beer, brewing, industry associations, pressure groups and the motives behind them, and start again by looking at the concept of "craft" in its own right.

Part Two:
"Craft Beer" is hopelessly misunderstood

Chapter 3:
The definition of "craft"

One day in January 2019, while I was browsing my local bookshop, I spotted *Craft: Why Traditional Handcrafts Are About More Than Just Making*, by Alexander Langlands. It struck me that it might be useful to look at craft from a different perspective. I was intrigued by the use of the Old English spelling, which struck me as pretentious and cool at the same time, just like craft beer can be. With the narcissism you get when you're too close to a subject, I wondered what Alexander Langlands would have to say about craft beer. But I was genuinely interested in learning more about traditional crafts such as haymaking and scything, so I could pretend to myself that I might one day move to the country and start doing that kind of thing, satisfying an itch to reconnect with slower, older rhythms that has been bugging me since I wrote *The Apple Orchard* (2016).

I flipped the book open. To enhance the handcrafted message of the text, the publisher begins each chapter with a woodcut-style illustration of the craft skill being discussed in that chapter. The pictures of haymakers, dry stone wallers, diggers and potters could be depicting craftspeople in any century from the middle ages to the present, and in that they encapsulate the entire point of the book. There's a preface entitled, "Why *Cræft*?" And the picture in front of this short chapter shows a burly man carefully pouring beer from a wooden barrel into a dimpled pint mug. I turned the page, and halfway down the first paragraph, Langlands writes, "A recent craze for craft beers means that we can consume craft and essentially come away with nothing to show for our purchase – except perhaps a slightly fuzzy head the next day".[34]

"Oh, this is brilliant!" I thought. "As part of this look at traditional craft skills we're going to get a perspective on the craft beer phenomenon from an expert on craft rather than an expert on beer!" I couldn't wait to see what Langlands had to say. Without looking any further, I paid my £20 and took the book home.

Langlands doesn't mention beer again throughout the entire book.

At first, I was disappointed. I started to revert to my usual position on beer coverage outside the beer writing bubble – or lack of it – fuming, "Why does no one treat beer with the respect it deserves? Brewing is way more of a craft than fucking *digging*, and there's a whole chapter on that!"

And then I calmed down, I read on, and I realised why.

If I'd read it properly when I first skimmed it, I would have understood that Alexander Langlands only mentions craft beer because, in his view, it is the perfect example of how over-used the word "craft" has become. He tells us there is "only the faintest overlap with the definition *craft* had when it first appeared in written English over a thousand years ago," and finishes that first page with the sentence, "It would seem that we can't quite put our finger on what *craeft* was".

Sound familiar?

"Craft has become so ubiquitous that it's increasingly difficult to state with any exactitude a definition precise enough to satisfy everyone,'[35] he continues. Definitional angst around craft is not just a beer problem. And if we

---

[34]Langlands, 2017, p.9.
[35]Ibid.

can't define "craft", how on earth can we expect to define "craft beer"?

Langlands, obviously, then goes on to write an entire chapter on the definition of *cræft*, using the Old English spelling of the word to create some space between his idea of what craft is and the miasma of modern usage of the term.

Peter Korn, a furniture maker and author of the beautiful short book *Why We Make Things and Why It Matters,* (2013) shares this concern over the difficulty in pinning craft down. "The word is a chameleon," he says. "It is both verb and noun. It is used to impute quality to everything from one-of-a-kind handmade objects to mass-produced industrial products… A lawyer may be said to craft an agreement with all the grammatical correctness with which a potter is said to craft a teacup. An actor practices his craft on the stage as readily as a blacksmith practices his at the forge".[36]

In *On Craftsmanship,* (2011) Christopher Frayling goes further, pointing out that 'craft' means different things in different contexts to different people:

> To a sociologist, the word 'craft' is associated with 'skilled manual labour', or 'the aristocracy of labour'. To an economist, with a stage in economic theory preceding capitalism… To an anthropologist, with the maker as user… To a countryman, with traditional rural pursuits. To a literary historian, with the anti-establishment stance of the Romantics. To a trade unionist, with a community of skilled people defending the way they perform their occupations. To a laboratory scientist, with the use of equipment to *do science*…'[37]

Frayling also returns to the point that craft can be a verb or a noun, and adds that the adverb "craftily" gives us yet

[36]Korn, Peter, *Why We Make Things And Why It Matters* (Vintage, London, 2017), p.30.
[37]Frayling, Christopher, *On Craftsmanship* (Oberon Books, London, 2017) p.10.

another angle on the word. To be "crafty" is to be deceitful and cunning, almost the opposite of the honest authenticity of craft itself. This slyness and deceitfulness can also be found in witchcraft, spycraft, and to some extent, statecraft.

The American Brewers' Association used this to great effect in 2012 when they deployed "crafty" to describe beers that presented themselves as craft, but deceived by doing so. "Is [your beer] a product of a small and independent brewer?" they asked the passionate beer lover, "Or is it from a crafty large brewer, seeking to capitalize on the mounting success of small and independent craft brewers?"[38]

There is a certain irony in this: until the nineteenth century, "crafty" referred to someone who was clever, dextrous and skilful. It then began to shift to describe an outsider, an anti-establishment agent who was using their cleverness, dexterity and skill to defy authority – a perfect description of the craft beer movement standing up to the Big Beer behemoths. We can join the dots pretty easily between "crafty" meaning a clever outsider beating the system, and "crafty" as being sly and untrustworthy.

Our struggles to define craft beer begin to look small by comparison, and, to some extent, irrelevant. The debate around the broader concept of craft rarely touches on issues of size or ownership of organisations, but instead expands to ultimately explore what it means to be human. And to get our heads around that – and to understand why the notion of craft is so difficult to pin down – we have to pop back to the Enlightenment.

Existential philosophy creates snobs of us all

As fans of Alexei Sayle will be aware, René Descartes was a very clever man. His philosophical proposition "I think,

---

[38]https://www.brewersassociation.org/press-releases/craft-vs-crafty-a-statement-from-the-brewers-association/

therefore I am," is one of the foundation stones of Western philosophy, and one of the few propositions of philosophy with which non-philosophers are familiar.

The full version of the proposition is a wonderful, tautological thought that I want to say sounds self-contradictory but is in fact the opposite: "I doubt, therefore I think, therefore I am". Descartes explained what he meant – and the significance of it – in his 1637 work *Discourse on Method*. He was exploring the notion that some of what we think we know may be fantasy, illusion, dream or fake – an idea that's still explored in stoned "what if we're all just figments of our dog's imagination?" type conversations, and films like *The Matrix*. Descartes's point was that if you are capable of doubting your own existence, this is itself proof that you *do* actually exist. If you can have doubts about your existence in the Matrix, that proves you are not simply a component of it, a non-player character created by it.

A very clever man indeed.

Descartes was a rationalist, trying to explain the mysteries of the world without necessarily falling back on religious doctrine. He was clearly fascinated by the nature of the human mind, which remains a mystery even today. We know what the brain is and what it does, but the mind itself is invisible, unmeasurable, undefinable. In 1641, Descartes proposed that mind and body were separate entities: the brain may be a physical object, but the mind is not. The mind is real, but it does not exist in physical space. As thinking creatures, we therefore exist as two separate entities: the mind and the body. As Descartes put it, "I have a clear and distinct idea of myself as a thinking, non-extended thing, and a clear and distinct idea of body as an extended and non-thinking thing".[39]

---

[39]Descartes, René (1641) "Meditations on First Philosophy", in *The Philosophical Writings of René Descartes*, trans. by J. Cottingham, R. Stoothoff and D. Murdoch, Cambridge:

Like Descartes's more famous proposition, this conception of the separation between mind and body, popularly known as "Cartesian Dualism", quickly took root in Western thought, and debates over it continue today. As the Enlightenment progressed, it created a dominant point of view that continues to have profound influence over how we perceive the nature of work.

Descartes believed that animals do not have minds and therefore cannot think. The mind is therefore the part of us that separates humans from animals, which means that the work of the mind is unique to us, whereas we can get animals – and later, simple, dumb machines – to do much physical labour for us.

Ever since the Enlightenment, not only have we made a distinction between mental and manual labour, we have placed mental labour above manual labour in a hierarchy of virtue. White-collar workers are seen as superior to blue-collar workers and earn more money (although this is no longer as true as it once was.) In the UK, we are all statistically catalogued on the ABC1C2E system of socio-demographic groups. Grade A is defined as "higher managerial, administrative or professional", B as being on the way there or working in a role supporting As. C1 is defined as "lower middle-class," referring to people who are in supervisory or clerical and junior managerial, administrative or professional jobs, while C2 is "skilled working-class" – referring to skilled manual workers – and D is straightforward working-class semi-skilled and unskilled manual labour. E refers to retired people, "casual and lowest grade workers," and the unemployed. It's a system that was defined in the 1930s, when most of Britain's population were skilled or unskilled manual workers. It's hopelessly outdated, but is still the primary form of social classification used across government and business today, helping to determine everything from what ads you see in your newspaper to how political parties target their messaging to win your vote.

This system of classification betrays a bias that's so ingrained, many of us don't even see it. In *Shop Class as Soulcraft*, (2009) Matthew Crawford argues that our educational system and our occupational structures are institutionally biased against manual labour, citing the term "knowledge worker" as the perfect example of our shift away from valuing actually being able to do stuff ourselves.[40] We are taught from primary school onwards to aspire, to better ourselves, to make our way up the socio-demographic ladder. Monty Python did a brilliant sketch that highlights these prejudices by subverting them. A successful London playwright (wearing mid-twentieth century manual labourer's clothes and speaking in a broad Yorkshire accent) receives a visit from his son (wearing a sharp suit and speaking in a posh, home counties accent) and the two get into a furious argument because the son has decided to forge a career coal-mining in the north instead of following in his father's footsteps. "Hampstead wasn't good enough for you was it? You had to go poncing off to Barnsley!"[41]

To imagine an extreme example that in some ways echoes the Python sketch, a master-craftsperson building violins, or a successful antique furniture repairer, are skilled working-class Ds, while the administrative staff they might employ to support them are middle-class and higher up the pecking order in C1 or even B. As Peter Korn points out, while the arts are classed as products of the mind, craft is seen as the work of the hands. As Christopher Frayling says while listing all the c-word's various definitional contexts:

---

[40]Crawford, Matthew, *Shop Class as Soulcraft: An Inquiry into the Value of Work*, (Penguin, New York, 2009) p.1. Published in the UK as *The Case For Working With Your Hands, or Why Office Work is Bad For Us and Fixing Things Feels Good*, (Penguin, London, 2009.)
[41]Monty Python's Flying Circus, Series One Episode 2, 1969 https://www.dailymotion.com/video/x32czn2

> To an art critic, the word 'craft' is about the distinction between an 'art' – as in intellectual/conceptual – and a 'mere craft' – as in a manual – a debased version of age-old debates about the social recognition of the artist which go back to the Italian Renaissance.[42]

Descartes's thinking helped solidify and codify thinking around craft that has roots as far back as Aristotle. Initially, in Ancient Greece, craftsmen were considered middle-class. In *The Odyssey*, Homer uses the term *demioergoi* to describe "those who work for the community".[43] This included skilled manual labourers such as potters, but also doctors, lower magistrates and professional singers. The *demioergoi* sat between the elite aristocracy and the mass of slaves whose work was considered to be unskilled. They all belonged to a group of people who had skills that benefitted others, and the distinction between manual and mental labour was not made.

Later, Aristotle was responsible for changing how we thought. In *Metaphysics*, he abandons *demioergoi* as a group that includes craftsmen, and calls them *cheirotechnon*, or "handworker" instead. The distinction is necessary, he argues, because "the architects in every profession are more estimable and know more and are wiser than the artisans, because they know the reasons of the things which are done".[44]

In the history of Western thought, knowing how to make useful stuff to a high standard has been made to seem inferior to loftier, intellectual pursuits ever since. This diminution has led to a fundamental misunderstanding of the nature of what we refer to as "manual labour" – a misunderstanding that was experienced, explored and encapsulated brilliantly by a Victorian teacher and aspiring

---

[42]Frayling, 2017, p.11.
[43]Quoted by Sennett, Richard, *The Craftsman* (Penguin, London, 2009) p22.
[44]Ibid. p.23.

writer called George Sturt.

Wheelwrights and wonder goals

George Sturt was a perfect example of the aspiration for betterment that Python so effectively lampooned. Born in Surrey in 1863, George was the son of Francis Sturt, a successful wheelwright. But he went to a grammar school, where he eventually became a pupil-teacher, and had ambitions to become a school inspector. But when Francis died in 1884, George, just into his twenties, felt obliged to take over the family business, which had been operating since 1704. In 1923, near the end of his life, he recounted his experience in *The Wheelwright's Shop*, a book he described as "an autobiography for the years 1884 to 1891", but which is still revered among fans of country and rural crafts as a loving evocation of lost skills and the world in which they were useful. That Sturt could write a whole book on how to make a wheel for a wooden wagon used by Surrey farmers in itself suggests that the distinction between mental and manual labour is somewhat simplistic. With whole chapters devoted to buying timber, sawing it, and seasoning it, Sturt confronts intellectual prejudices head on.

While he had done odd jobs as a child for his father, Sturt hadn't spent the seven-year apprenticeship learning the wheelwright's trade that was common for youths destined to enter it. He knew he was a clever bloke, so he initially assumed he'd be able to pick up everything he needed to know:

> With the idea that I was going to learn everything from the beginning I put myself eagerly to boys' jobs, not at all dreaming that, at over twenty, the nerves and muscles are no longer able to put on the cell-growths, and so acquire the habits of perceiving and doing, which should have begun at fifteen. Could not Intellect achieve it?[45]

---

[45]Sturt, George, *The Wheelwright's Shop* (Cambridge University Press, Cambridge, 1930) Ch.11.

But it wasn't just a case of not being physically developed enough. He thought that the tasks themselves were simple. There's an underlying assumption that if you are bright, then the tasks of supposedly less intelligent people will be easy to understand. Sturt thought he'd quickly be able to pick up the entire skill base of the wheelwright:

> I was trying to learn four or five trades at once; and "intellect" fooled me by making them look simple. Indeed, so much of hand-work as intellect can understand does have that appearance, almost always to the undoing of the book-learned, who grow conceited. How simple is coal-hewing, fiddling, fishing, digging, to the student of books! I thought my business looked easy.[46]

Sturt instead learns very quickly that there are different kinds of knowledge: that which can be taught from books, and that which can only be acquired from experience:

> In fact, Intellect made but a fumbling imitation of real knowledge, yet hardly deigned to recognise how clumsy in fact it was. Beginning so late in life I know now I could never have earned my keep as a skilled workman…[47]

"Manual labour" isn't just manual at all. Skilled manual labour relies on knowledge that is learned through experience, and then experienced as instinctive. In truth, it seems to have little to do with instinct, and everything to do with a different kind of learning that doesn't get enough credit from societies that prize intellect above all else. Sociologists distinguish between "formal" knowledge and "tacit" knowledge, the former being characterised as set down in books and easy to communicate, the latter being difficult to articulate in speech or writing. It's the difference between knowledge and know-how, between knowing the capital of France and knowing how to tie your shoelaces. You learn the former by reading. The latter is the result of practice and repetition, in some ways more difficult to learn,

---

[46]Ibid.
[47]Ibid.

and certainly more difficult to teach, describe or explain.

In *The Craftsman,*(2009)[48] , Richard Sennett credits Denis Diderot's *Encyclopédie, ou dictionnaire raisonné des sciences, des arts et des métiers (Encyclopedia, or a Systematic Dictionary of the Sciences, Arts, and Crafts)* with placing manual labour back on an even footing with mental work, over a century before George Sturt first entered his father's workshop.

Written between 1751 and 1772, the *Encyclopédie* aimed to capture all the world's knowledge and to secularise learning away from the Jesuits. Given the nature of his task, it wasn't long before Diderot encountered the difficulty of trying to describe and encapsulate tacit knowledge. Visiting workshops and asking craftsmen to describe what they were doing, he found that, "Among a thousand one will be lucky to find a dozen who are capable of explaining the tools or machinery they use, and the things they produce, with any clarity". No problem, he thought, I'll just learn these crafts myself and then I'll be able to describe them. But this proved more difficult than he thought, prompting a new respect for craftsmen and their talents.

Another example closer to my heart is the best England goal I've witnessed in my lifetime. In the 1996 European Cup, England faced Scotland in Group A. Paul Gascoigne is running forward and the ball reaches him just outside the box. One Scottish defender is rapidly closing to his left, another to his right. With one touch, he loops the ball over the head of the right-hand defender, Colin Hendry. As the ball falls from its arc, with a second touch, he fires it into the top-right corner of the net. "I could see Colin Hendry coming in," he later told *FourFourTwo* magazine. "So I flicked it over his head [with his left foot] and volleyed it [with his right]. You can't teach kids that, it was pure instinct."

---

[48]Sennett, 2009, pp90-106.

As someone who struggles to kick a football without tripping over it, I'm reluctant to contradict Gascoigne. But what he refers to as "instinct" is a combination of an intimate knowledge of his opponent's behaviour (he'd been a team-mate of Hendry's at Rangers) his own body's capabilities, and a tacit understanding of how air pressure, gravity, inertia and momentum combine to influence the aerodynamics of a leather sphere in motion, and how to judge the correct degree and angle of force applied to that sphere to make it do exactly what he wanted. Gazza couldn't possibly explain any of this verbally – and neither could any other footballer without a degree in physics. Gascoigne was routinely ridiculed throughout his career for being stupid. Although Richard Sennett isn't talking about Gascoigne here, he explains perfectly why this is wrong, a product of our inbuilt bias towards knowledge over know-how:

> Inarticulate does not mean stupid; indeed what we can say in words may be more limited than what we do with things. Craftwork establishes a realm of skill and knowledge perhaps beyond human verbal capacities to explain; it taxes the powers of the most professional writer to describe precisely how to tie a slipknot... language is not an adequate 'mirror tool' for the physical movements of the human body.[49]

Whether or not you believe it is essential that "craft" must involve working with the hands (or feet), it's inarguable that it also involves the mind, even if we can't quite articulate how. The Cartesian separation of mind and body may be an interesting philosophical conundrum, but it hinders our understanding of what craft is. Mind and body may be different, but they're two aspects of the same thing and one cannot work without the other.

The man who first coined the term craft – or *cræft* – knew this all along. Alfred the Great – or *Ælfræd* if we're going to be consistent now we've started this *æ* thing – was King of

---

[49]Ibid., p95.

Wessex from 871 to 886 and then King of the Anglo-Saxons from 886 to 899. He was the first to translate classical Latin texts into Old English. As he did so, he added his own comments and insights. With Old English having a more limited capacity than Latin, Alfred has to make it work hard to cover the ideas he's exploring, and the word he pushes harder than any other is *cræft*. According to Langlands, Alfred uses it to describe "a quality or state of being; an almost indefinable knowledge or wisdom".[50] The term crops up 1331 times in all Anglo-Saxon documents, and its most common use is to evoke "power or skill in the context of knowledge, ability and a kind of learning. Furthermore, a sense of mental skill – merit, talent or excellence – occurs as many times as the sense of mere physical skill".[51]

This is why craft is at once tricksier and more useful than its French counterpart, *artisanale*. Sennett argues that while *artisanale*, and its German counterpart, *handwerk*, are explicitly and exclusively related to manual work, "craft" is more open, acknowledging the role of the mind, which is why we can have *statecraft*. Whereas Langlands, even after reading Alfred, still believes that craft must involve the movement of the human body, and Frayling gives a "common sense" definition of the word as "An activity that involves skill in making things by hand",[52] Sennett argues that craft is far more than skilled manual labour and can apply to any profession: "The carpenter, lab technician and [orchestra] conductor are all craftsmen".[53]

But Sennett still believes that even if you're a lab technician or the conductor of an orchestra, the physical part of those jobs, the involvement of the body and how you move it while working, are important. He argues that when head and

---

[50]Langlands, 2017, p17.
[51]Ibid.
[52]Frayling, 2017, p9.
[53]Sennett, 2009, p.20.

hand are separated, the head suffers – our understanding and our means of expression are compromised. When head and hand are unified, "Forms of mental understanding emerge from developing specialised and rarefied hand skills, whether these be playing perfectly in tune, cleaving a grain of rice, or blowing a difficult goblet. But even such virtuoso skills are based on fundamentals of the human body".[54]

Nicer than it has to be

Peter Korn talks of "materiality", how "The maker sees the immediate effect of every step he takes along the way. When his work is concluded, the fruit of his labour stands there, unambiguously".[55]

The rewards of this are greater than we initially may think. According to Sennett, "The emotional rewards craftsmanship holds out for attaining skill are twofold: people are anchored in tangible reality, and they can take pride in their work".[56] But both writers then go further. We know ourselves better when we feel more connected to our physical bodies, and we make sense of the world by physically interacting with it.

With this understanding – that craft is about a unity of skills, and the personal satisfaction gained from using those skills to create something – Sennett has no problem giving a clear and concise definition of craft, as "A basic human impulse, the desire to do a job well for its own sake".[57]

This sits very closely next to a thought that's been preoccupying me for several years. Whenever I experience a sense of pleasure, even delight, from everyday things, be that choosing a sandwich for lunch, interacting with a

---

[54]Ibid. p.178.
[55]Korn, 2017, p.55.
[56]Sennett, 2009, p.21.
[57]Ibid. p.9.

cashier or member of bar staff, or admiring beautiful architecture, the single thought that's common to every experience is: *This is nicer than it absolutely needs to be.* Compare the grandeur of a Victorian railway station with the brutal glass and metal tube monstrosities springing in up in places like Derby and Oxford, which seem to be designed to create a hostile environment for travellers; or the dreary malaise of a packaged egg mayonnaise sandwich from one of the concessions on those station platforms with one made fresh by the owner of an independent café. It seems that as we supposedly become more affluent as a society, our everyday experience is being pared back and stripped down, through a combination of fashion, a relentless pursuit of cost-cutting, and a simple can't-be-arsedness that comes from feeling none of the emotional rewards of craftsmanship in our various jobs.

Given then that craft is about labour, about what we do and how we feel when we work, it's unsurprising that interest in the broader area of craft spikes in relation to the changing nature of work. When we find ourselves feeling alienated by what we do for a living, we re-evaluate it. In the third decade of the twenty-first century, this process is accelerating. In the UK, the first few months of 2020 saw a debate about the government's new policy of preventing immigrants from coming into the country to do "unskilled" jobs. When the details were announced, every newspaper report I saw used a photograph of bar, pub or restaurant staff to illustrate what it meant by "unskilled", prompting me to write in a magazine column, "I'd love to see Priti Patel trying to clean a cask line, or Dominic Cummings keep his cool behind a city centre bar at 10.45pm on the last Friday before Christmas".[58]

The newspapers could have used any of the other jobs –

---

[58] https://www.morningadvertiser.co.uk/Article/2020/02/24/If-I-were-a-bar-person-or-waiter-I-d-be-profoundly-insulted-by-the-use-of-the-term-unskilled-labour

bricklayers, builders, decorators, fruit pickers – that the British government currently counts as unskilled, and been just as wrong. And then, just two months later, we began to re-evaluate how we thought of nurses, delivery drivers, supermarket checkout staff, and all the other jobs that had suddenly become "front line".

On the morning I write this, there's an article in *The Guardian* headlined, "Coronavirus is teaching the UK it's wrong to deride the practical professions". In it, Liz Lightfoot argues for a radical rethink of how we treat the jobs that are seen as inferior to "professional" work:

> We don't need only doctors, lawyers, civil servants, accountants and money analysts. We are crying out for care workers, plumbers, electricians and car mechanics. We applaud manufacturers who change tack to make ventilators and face masks. We are prostrate with gratitude to those keeping some semblance of normality going – the supermarket cashiers, bus and train drivers, and the refuse collectors. Oh, how we miss our hairdressers as we battle to disguise our greying locks.[59]

We'll come back later to the growing interest in working with our hands as a way to reconnect with the world around us by doing a job well for its own sake. But first, we'll go back to the first time this happened, and the roots of our modern understanding of "craft" not just as a word, but a movement.

---

[59]https://www.theguardian.com/education/2020/apr/21/coronavirus-is-teaching-the-uk-its-wrong-to-deride-the-practical-professions

Chapter 4:
The democratisation of beauty

Life moves pretty fast

The closing decades of the nineteenth century saw a technological revolution in the brewing industry that was unprecedented. Brewing – for so long considered an art or craft – was being taken over by science. Within our discussion of craft, it's important to note that, at the time, it was brewers – not accountants or marketers – who were leading this.

You may enjoy a sour beer these days. You might be fascinated by the stories of wild yeasts and the unique character they bring to beer, and bored of consistently clean beers that are the same one after another. That boredom is a privilege that, in the context of beer's 10,000-year history, has been around for less than a century and a half.

In 1842, a new beer style was created in the Czech town of Plžen. It was light and refreshing, and Plžen sat at the heart of the Austrian Empire – a huge single market. In ensuing decades, the arrival of rail transport and refrigeration helped pilsner beer spread with lightning speed across Europe. The *Reinheitsgebot*-loving Germans found it to be a perfect expression of their art, and given that the brewers in Plžen had copyrighted neither the style nor the name of their new beer, pilsner became a German style too. When the political upheaval of the Franco-Prussian War (1870-71) and German unification led to mass emigration to the United States, pilsner beer went along for the ride. Frederick Miller, Eberhard Anheuser, Augustus Busch, Joseph Schlitz and Frederick Pabst are merely the most famous names who took advantage of the barley from America's vast farm belt to build brewing businesses that were so successful that they replaced hard cider – the drink America was founded upon – with lager in a few short decades.

The Franco-Prussian war also changed the course of brewing history in another fundamental way. In the wake of a humiliating French defeat, Louis Pasteur decided to share his ground-breaking work on the actions of yeasts with English ale brewers, encouraging them to buy microscopes and analyse their beers, showing not only how yeast was the agent of fermentation, but also how other micro-organisms caused spoilage. Emil Hansen at Carlsberg built on Pasteur's work by isolating single strain yeasts and cultivating them in the laboratory. One of his successors at Carlsberg, Niels Hjelte Claussen, would later analyse older British ale styles to determine the special quality that separated them from beers that had been using Pasteur's methods, and discover the presence of a wilder relative to brewing yeast which he named the "British fungus", or *Brettanomyces*.

Laboratories became commonplace in breweries, but not everyone was comfortable with them. The presence of scientific equipment suggested to visitors that the beer was being "doctored" or adulterated – a common practice among less scrupulous brewers. Horace Tabberer Brown, a scientific brewer who started work at Burton's Worthington Brewery in 1866, later described how his boss "was of the old school" and resisted the use of chemical apparatus to analyse the town's famous brewing water. "A compromise was reached whereby a small room was later fitted with a balance and apparatus for water analysis, but the little office in which these were placed for my use had its windows carefully obscured so that no one could see what was going on inside".[60]

---

[60]https://web.archive.org/web/20110716130951/http://www.scientificsocieties.org/jib/papers/1919/1919BrownHoraceLecture.pdf

Science and technology were transforming brewing. Those brewers, such as Heineken, Carlsberg, Bass and Budweiser, who were already big enough and rich enough to invest in the equipment needed to capitalise on these new methods, grew even bigger, and it's here that the seeds of the future global brewing monoliths were planted. But it's important to state that, for now at least, science and technology were objectively improving the quality of beer, not making it worse. That would come later, after falling volumes of beer and the rise of big brand marketing displaced the brewer in the hierarchy of business decision making.

Nevertheless, as Horace Brown illustrates, there was deep suspicion among those who adored beer that a millennia-old craft was being mucked around with by all this new equipment and methodology. It wasn't natural. Couldn't we just go back to how things were?

This was an attitude that, in the 1880s and 1890s, spread well beyond beer. Charles Dickens began his writing career in the 1840s by celebrating the central role of the stagecoach and coaching inn in *The Pickwick Papers*. By the end of it, he was witnessing trains scream through smog-choked London. He was vague about the times his novels were set, but often seemed to locate them about twenty years before whenever he was writing them. When the present speeds up – until the simple act of living can feel like you're in the cabin of a steam train that's speeding out of control – the past becomes a source of reassurance and stability. We revise things that happened at the time because we have hindsight: we can see how they turned out, and that gives us a feeling of control and balance.

The Victorian Age therefore gave birth to the myth of Merrie England, of Robin Hood and his merry men, thatched cottages, morris dancers, ribbon-bedecked maypoles and country fayres. Much of our perception of Britain, particularly England, between the Middle Ages and the Industrial Revolution was an invention – or at best, a gross distortion – by nostalgic Victorians seeking continuity and reassurance. It's a myth that to this day informs our perception of craft.

The comforting myth of craft

Many writers on craft characterise it as a knowledge that is lost to us, or in the process of being lost; skills that we used to take for granted but no longer need, yet feel diminished that we no longer have them. Alexander Langlands describes *craft* as "the indefinable intelligence of our Anglo-Saxon forebears", and blames its decline on industrialisation, cheap power, and our ability to do things at the flick of a switch that used to take a lot of effort. Once, it would have been pretty fundamental for an English man to be proficient with an axe. Few of us are today. But a few years ago, while driving through a heavily wooded part of South Wales with my friend Bill, I suddenly remembered, after a thirty-year gap, that while in scouts I had learned how and when to use a hand axe, trimming axe and felling axe. As the knowledge returned of how to fell a tree safely and efficiently, and make it fall in the direction I want it to, I felt blissfully happy – not because I will ever need to fell a tree again, but just because I *know*, and because I appreciate that we wouldn't have reached the point where we no longer need to know if generations of people hadn't known before us.

It's a sentiment that's summed up by the traditional Saxony spinning wheel many of us probably encountered for the first time in childhood stories of Rumpelstiltskin and Sleeping Beauty, spinning straw into gold or poisoning a princess into a hundred-year sleep. This big, wooden, friendly-looking wheel has become a staple image in the shop signs, logos and windows of countless craft shops around the world, a near-universal symbol of handcrafted quality and simplicity, of honest manufacture. It implies that industrial production has taken something from us, and we're going to get it back – a familiar narrative to anyone who has been moved by what CAMRA campaigns for. The spinning wheel is a powerful image that fills us with longing for a time of happy artisans creating products using traditional methods and their customers admiring the craftsmanship, of ancient skills handed down through generations in a timeless rural idyll now lost to us.

But if it makes you feel any better, like Merrie England, this time of happy craftsmen and women never really existed in the first place – at least, not as we imagine it now.

Before the Industrial Revolution, the skills we now consider to be crafts were not thought of in a distinct or special way – they were simply how things were done. When new techniques or better tools came along, they were quickly adopted – the Industrial Revolution was simply an acceleration of a constant process of innovation.

More importantly, it's been estimated that less than ten percent of the UK population were engaged in trades that could be described as craftsmanship – the vast majority were peasants performing menial tasks. Robert Blauner, in his book *Work Satisfaction and Industrial Trends,* claims the typical medieval worker was "practically nothing more than a working beast".[61]

In reality, the Industrial Revolution never deskilled a population of happy artisans: most of us never had those skills in the first place. Our modern idea of craftsmanship, and of the skills and values it entails, didn't exist before the Industrial Revolution created it. Craft was born as a direct reaction to the Industrial Revolution, and grew up as a concept alongside it, as what Langlands refers to as "a self-conscious counter-point to factory-made goods".[62]

---

[61]Blauner, Richard, *Work Satisfaction and Industrial Trends in Modern Society* (University of California, 1960) quoted in Frayling, 2017, pp. 64-65.
[62]Langlands, 2017, p.12.

The Arts & Crafts Movement of the late nineteenth and early twentieth centuries was itself the product of the increasing affluence created by the industrial era. One of its leading lights, William Morris, was born to a wealthy family in Walthamstow in 1834, which turned out to be about 500 years too late for him. As a child he had his own suit of armour, and a big garden in which to live out his medieval fantasies. He studied Classics at Oxford, where he quickly grew bored of the way it was taught and drifted further into medievalism, bonding with friends such as Edward Burne-Jones over a shared love of Tennyson and Arthurian legend. He also discovered the writings of painter, poet and art critic John Ruskin.

Ruskin was something of a medievalist himself, and in particular championed the gothic style of architecture. In volume two of his work *The Stones of Venice* (1851), he argued that Gothic ornament was a true expression of an artisan's joy in free, creative work, in words that foreshadow future debates on the meaning of craft:

> We want one man to be always thinking, and another to be always working, and we call one a gentleman, and the other an operative; whereas the workman ought often to be thinking, and the thinker often to be working, and both should be gentlemen, in the best sense. As it is, we make both ungentle, the one envying, the other despising, his brother; and the mass of society is made up of morbid thinkers and miserable workers. Now it is only by labour that thought can be made healthy, and only by thought that labour can be made happy, and the two cannot be separated with impunity.[63]

This part of *The Stones of Venice* had a profound impact on Morris, who called it "one of the very few necessary and inevitable utterances of the century".[64]

---

[63]Ruskin, John, *The Stones of Venice*, (1851) Volume II, ChapterVI, paragraph xxi, accessed via Project Gutenburg http://www.gutenberg.org/ebooks/9804
[64]Morris, William, "Preface to The Nature of Gothic by John Ruskin," accessed via

Looking around the Morris Museum in Walthamstow, there's a lot of naivety in the young William's medieval obsession. The group he formed around himself, which included Burne-Jones, Dante Gabriel Rossetti and Neo-Gothic architect Philip Webb, initially reminded me of any group of young men fresh out of uni who think they are the first to discover what's truly important in life. But over time, Morris's ideas develop, and he displays both a talent for learning and capacity for work across architecture, interior decoration, poetry, education, craftsmanship, prose and political activism that are astonishing. When he died in 1896, his doctor said, "The cause was simply being William Morris and having done more work than most ten men".[65]

Over that busy life, he was the chief architect of the Arts & Crafts movement, which ultimately became a synthesis of his myriad interests. Medievalism was honed into a sharper critique of the industrial age, which had created overcrowded slums, epidemic diseases and environmental pollution. As he grew older, he became more interested in direct socialist activism as a way of combatting society's ills. But he began with a mission to democratise art and beauty. "I do not want art for a few, any more than education for a few, or freedom for a few," he said in 1877.[66]

Morris believed the way to do this was to give back to artists and craftsmen the dignity and job satisfaction that the Industrial Revolution had stolen from them. Mechanisation had reduced work to mindless, repetitive tasks. More importantly, it had taken away from workers any sense of control or direction over how the products of their labour would turn out. Morris believed this diminished both the worker and the objects they made. He created workshops in which standardised tasks were recombined and craftsmen

https://www.marxists.org/archive/morris/works/index.htm
[65]Quoted on a display at the William Morris Gallery, Walthamstow, North London. https://wmgallery.org.uk
[66]Ibid.

were given autonomy over the results. The aesthetic was folksy and innocent, the style practical and beautiful. In 1881, Morris moved his workshops to Merton Abbey in Surrey. Photos of the workshops show a spacious, calm, ramshackle working environment that was as far away as Morris could conceive from the industrial factories he described as "nightmare buildings" and "temples of overcrowding and overwork".[67]

If you want a clearer picture of what this working environment was like, you need only watch *The Repair Shop*, a long-running BBC series available in the UK on iPlayer. The show is filmed at the Weald and Downland Living Museum near Chichester, West Sussex, in the heart of typically telegenic rolling English countryside. The museum teaches "traditional trades and crafts to ensure their preservation and [shares] the untold stories of rural life and those who lived it in the South East of England".[68]

The Repair Shop is not a permanent fixture at the museum, but a creation of TV producers. But within the context of the programme, this is an almost magical place where saintly craftspeople, with a mastery of all manner of skills from clock-making to weaving to carpentry, repair broken heirlooms and antiques brought in by viewers who always have a story to tell around each object.

In some ways then, *The Repair Shop* has all the contrivance and artifice of any reality TV show. But the appeal of the programme is in the calm skill of the repairers. I'm particularly fascinated by the close-ups of their hands as they work. I cannot believe how steady and deliberate their movements are, how *safe* each object and its sometimes-tiny parts look in their care. The work is slow and steady, and the results are always beyond the hopes of the item's owners. Beyond the manual skills being shown in close-up,

[67]Ibid.
[68]https://www.wealddown.co.uk

the viewer is often struck by a sense of "What? But how the hell did you know that that's how the speedometer of a 1920s car used to work?" Each show demonstrates perfectly the union of hand and head. It's plausible that some of the objects featured could have been made originally by similar craftsmen in Morris's own workshops, and with cutaways to sheep gambolling and birds nesting in the trees, the contrast with any factory – Victorian or modern – could not be starker.

It would take a cold, dead heart to question Morris or Ruskin over their ideals and intentions. But from the outset, the Arts & Crafts Movement was fraught with as much paradox and irony as our recent attempts to define craft beer. Ruskin fetishized physical work, having never had to work as a labourer himself. He was keenly aware of this irony, and attempted to resolve it in 1874, while he was the first Slade Professor of Fine Art at Oxford, by asking some of his students to help him finish the building of a country road to replace a swampy track. Echoing again the craft movement's opposition to the division of mental and physical labour, he wrote:

> We keep a certain number of clowns digging and ditching, and generally stupefied, in order that we, being fed gratis, may have all the thinking and feeling to ourselves. Let a man once learn to take a straight shaving off a plank, or draw a fine curve without faltering, or lay a brick level in its mortar, and he has learned a multitude of other matters which no lips of man could teach him.[69]

And so Ruskin took his Oxford undergrads – including a young Oscar Wilde – to dig and lay stones under the supervision of his gardener and handyman, whom he referred to as "The Professor of Digging," and they all had a jolly time, with other students coming to watch and remark on how cool and edgy this was, until it was the end of term

---

[69] John Ruskin, "Sesame of Kings' Treasuries", quoted in Frayling, 2017, p. 84.

and Ruskin went to Venice, and the students to their respective pursuits, and the road faded from existence.

It's not difficult to imagine what full-time road workers, with no option of returning to the cloisters when they got a blister or felt a bit tired, would have made of all this. As one biographer of Ruskin observed, "Ruskin's admiration for the qualities he saw in physical work has been widely shared, particularly by those who are not called upon to do very much of it".[70]

The uncomfortable truths of craft

Ruskin's views on the meaningfulness of work throw up other difficult questions. He believed that the true value of a building or object is derived from the pleasure in creating it. [71] But who gets to define what true value is, and what other notions of value are false? Because I must admit, if I'm spending money on a car, a laptop or an oven, the most important notion of value to me is that it works and is safe. I truly hope that the people who made it got some fulfilment from doing so, but when I think about it, I'm guessing they possibly didn't. Millions of us feel uncomfortable with the idea of objects being produced in sweatshops in Eastern Asia, but not enough to stop buying them. Who can say an iPhone doesn't have value because the people who made it were probably miserable? And if you think that's a horrible question to ask, don't blame me, blame John Ruskin. He started it.

I'm citing Ruskin out of context to make a point: there's a truth at the heart of Arts & Crafts that is laudable in intent but uncomfortable in the wider world – craft is inherently selfish. That's not necessarily a bad thing; we just need to understand it for what it is – namely, the belief that, at the

---

[70]Anthony, PD, *John Ruskin's Labour*, quoted in Frayling, 2017, p.86
[71]Ruskin discussed by Langlands, 2017, p.28

very least, work should have some degree of dignity and satisfaction, and at best, should be a source of meaning and fulfilment for the craftsperson. This is the central idea of Peter Korn's book on craftsmanship, in which he argues that "we practise contemporary craft as a process of self-transformation".[72] This is *not* born of a desire to supply customers with a better standard of craft objects. Morris's desire to make art and beauty accessible to all soon faded in relation to his desire to make work meaningful and fulfilling for the maker. If these crafted objects make people like the customers at *The Repair Shop* happy, that's great. But that isn't the main motivation of the craft movement – not even close to it. Korn goes even further by suggesting that, given that people can easily buy non-crafted objects that are useful, modern-day craft doesn't actually have to any practical value at all:

> Premodern craft was made to satisfy culturally prescribed functional purposes. A hatbox held a hat, a snuff box held snuff, a clothes press held clothes. Contemporary craft, being economically marginal, is created primarily to address the spiritual needs of its maker. As a result, it often lacks utility and its practical disposition may be left to the whim of the purchaser.[73]

This leads us directly to the second uncomfortable truth about craft – uncomfortable at least from the point of view of the consumer – craft is elitist.

This is why the Arts & Crafts movement ultimately collapsed over its various irreconcilable ambitions: by placing the dignity and job-satisfaction of the worker above all else and ensuring they were paid a fair price for their labour, Arts & Crafts objects *had* to sell at a higher price than mass-produced industrial products. Only the wealthy could afford to buy them. And who were the wealthiest? The industrialists who owned the factories turning out the bog-standard stuff that was affordable to the masses.

---

[72]Korn, 2017, p.104
[73]Ibid. p.30.

Chrisopher Frayling gives the perfect example of this irony in an essay about skill. The Saxony spinning wheel we discussed earlier, probably the most potent image of craft in its broadest sense, dates back to the late fifteenth century and had long been obsolete by the nineteenth. It was a common sight in Victorian drawing rooms, but its primary purpose was as a symbolic piece of furniture:

> The fashion for home spinning in Victorian times had much more to do with the desire of second-generation industrialists to pretend their wealth had nothing to do with industry, than… with the genuine survival of a craft. The Victorian spinning wheel, about which we are encouraged to become so nostalgic, was to a large extent nostalgic in the first place, a symbol of status rather than of craft survival. And a way of 'making things' as a leisure occupation.[74]

Alexander Langlands recognises the same problem, and completes the circle:

> In a cycle of contradictory irony, the captains of industry used Arts & Crafts objects to overtly display their wealth and status, while the captains of Arts & Crafts relied on industrial money for their patronage.[75]

Coming at this from the perspective of craft beer, I experienced an almost knee-jerk reaction urging me to accuse the Arts & Crafts movement of selling out to The Man. But looking at the history of crafted products, it was always thus. Throughout history, successful craftspeople – and successful artists – have always had rich patrons paying the bills. Initially, any great artist in Europe earned their fortune by taking commissions from the Catholic Church. Medieval and Renaissance craftspeople, working through powerful guilds, were employed by courtiers and nobility to build houses and palaces where the whole point of their skill was to make these places as grand as possible compared to the hovels most people lived in.

---

[74]Frayling, 2017, p.68.
[75]Langlands, 2017, p.29.

There were always patrons. By the nineteenth century, only the occupation of the customer had changed. What's the point in making something fine if no one's going to buy it? Without people paying for it, it's just a hobby – as so much craft activity is today. Shakespeare is simply the best-known of all the writers who opened a famous work with a letter of thanks to their patron, often describing this benefactor in terms of the most fulsome praise. Rather than selling out on some great ideal, Arts & Crafts never "sold in" in the first place. It gave dignity back to a select group of craftspeople, but it utterly failed to deflect the onward march of industrialisation and standardisation, undone by the incompatibility of its early aims to democratise art and beauty even for the poorest in society, while maintaining that those who made it should be paid handsomely.

The Arts & Crafts movement existed within the system it reacted against, and was dependent upon that system for its survival. The first Arts & Crafts Exhibition was held in 1888 at the New Gallery in London's Regent Street, with the aim of reflecting "an intellectual engagement with how making fits into society, culture and economy".[76] It's pretty clear from that who the target audience were – and who they were not. While the Exhibition was successful in significantly broadening the range of different arts and crafts that were being exhibited, this marble-bedecked and gilded palace arguably has more chance of bringing beauty into the lives of normal people today, as Burberry's London flagship store.

But for all its flaws, and considering it was a spent force by 1920, the defeat of the Arts & Crafts movement was a glorious one. It may have done nothing to change the onward march of industrialised production, but it left behind the idea of a counter-cultural alternative to the mainstream that still rumbles through our culture a century later. Before it, if the word "craft" had cropped up in a

[76]Ibid.

word association game, the most likely answer would have been "witch". Now, when we think of craft, or crafts, we think of it in the terms the Arts & Crafts movement defined and popularised. Whether "craft" makes you think of crochet or carving, wood-turning or basket-weaving, as Peter Korn argues, this conceptualisation of craft became so powerful that it "permeated the public mind [to the extent] that the making of most non-art, non-manufactured objects throughout history came to be called craft in retrospect."[77] Morris and co. didn't just define craft in their present day; they shaped its future, and rewrote its past, defining its powerful appeal as well as its definitional flaws and paradoxes.

That appeal, and its accompanying definitional flaws, will feel instantly familiar to anyone reading about the Arts & Crafts movement from the perspective of modern craft beer. If you are, the most fascinating aspect of the whole story is that ownership and independence – the core tenets of modern craft beer – are barely mentioned.

While there is an assumption that craftspeople will be working on a small scale, possibly even on their own in a studio or garret, the specific concept of who owns the place doesn't seem relevant to the broader idea of craft. The craftsperson may be independent in their attitude. If they're any good, they almost certainly have their own independent aesthetic, their trademark look and feel, and they are definitely keen to express their own identity on the medium in which they work. But a craft furniture maker takes a commission from someone who has a lot of money. They design that piece of furniture according to the wishes and needs of the person paying the money. Any craftsperson always has.

The Arts & Crafts movement teaches us about the contradictions and paradoxes that run through any

---

[77]Korn, 2017, p.36.

conversation about the notion of craft. Maybe we can take some comfort in that the frustrations among beer fans around the topic of craft beer are not just created by us debating something meaningless inside a bubble, but are endemic in the whole idea of craft more broadly.

But at the same time, this broader contemplation of the history and meaning of craft as an idea that stands in direct opposition to the ideology of industrialised, mechanised production also starts to lead us away from thinking about ownership and independence, and prompts me to want to explore in much greater detail the way that things are made – and the skill, freedom and motivation of the people who are making them.

Chapter 5:
The technology tree

Roll out the barrel

Like most people whose idea of "working with your hands" extends to tapping a keyboard, I remain eternally terrified of being humiliated by skilled manual labourers and craftspeople. In *Pie Fidelity* (2019) I wrote about the terror of going to a DIY shop and trying to front it out, pretending you know what you're talking about. Every time someone comes to the house to fix the washing machine or boiler, I inwardly revert to my 14-year-old self, awkward and nervous, hopelessly inadequate.

There's one particular example of this that sticks in my mind. Whatever you think of their beers, Marston's in Burton-on-Trent is my favourite brewery to visit. This is chiefly because of the Burton Unions – massive rows of wooden barrels held together horizontally in sets of six, each set with a shallow metal trough resting above it, with swan-neck pipes from the barrels sputtering fermenting suds into the trough, the frothy yeast remaining there while the beer drains back into the barrels below. If that sounds weird or difficult to comprehend, that's because it is. These union sets were ubiquitous in Burton when it was the most important brewing town on the planet. They are now unique to Marston's.[78]

---

[78] It's taking all my writing discipline not to wax lyrical about the Burton Unions here, but I have written about them in detail many times before. For a full description of what they are, how they work and what they do, and why this makes Marston's in many ways the quintessential craft brewery, please see Brown, Pete *Miracle Brew* (Unbound, London, 2017).

These Burton Unions are in near-constant use, and this means Marston's is one of the last breweries in the world to employ a full-time cooper to maintain and repair the wooden barrels.

Coopering is where the notion of craft beer and the broader concept of craft directly intersect. Beer geeks in general are besotted by wooden barrels and beers that have been aged in them, and barrel-making is a perfect example of everything we have discussed about craftsmanship. Mark Newton, the master cooper at Burton, began his apprenticeship in 1977, aged seventeen. His workshop contains tools he's had since then, some of them worn to the shape of his hand. He has tools that are at least a hundred years old, and tools whose origin has been lost, each in its particular place on racks around his workshop, which sits just behind the Burton Union rooms.

I've no idea how many brewery tours Mark has demonstrated the art of coopering to, but I've seen his routine at least three times, and each time I'm fascinated and slightly scared. Famously, there is no measurement in coopering: the only tools Mark doesn't seem to possess are tape measures and spirit levels. Everything is done by hand and eye, which is why coopering simply can't be done without a five-year apprenticeship.

Most of Mark's tools are variations on planes or lathes, each one shaped to a single specific task in constructing a barrel. It would take me a year of that apprenticeship just to learn their many excellent names.

"Now I'm just going to use the adze," Mark will say, or "For this bit we get the croze," or "Now we need the stoup plane".

That's where my fascination with Mark's coopering demo comes from. The fear relates to the time he demonstrated how you start making a barrel by gathering a bunch of loose staves inside the first iron hoop and making them stand independently as a loose structure. Once, after showing how it was done, Mark invited me to have a go. I got as far as holding two staves against the hoop in one hand, and trying to add a third and a fourth, wondering how the hell I was going to keep them in place while I reached for a fifth, before the whole lot clattered to the workshop floor. I guess I must have tried about ten times before gently being asked to stop so we could get on with the demonstration, and I never got any further. Mark Newton might as well have been an Olympic high-jump medallist demonstrating how to clear a world record height, then asking me to repeat what he'd just done.

Craftsmanship is undoubtedly about skill developed to a high level. But what is skill? Christopher Frayling calls it "A word to start an argument with",[79] and spends many pages exploring the concept, pondering, "Does it refer to manual dexterity, craft experience, conceptual activity, general know-how, or a shifting combination of these four?"[80]

The relation between different types, or even different elements, of skill does shift. When I was trying to make the staves of the barrel stand up, I was using my recent memory of having watched Mark do the same, and a hundred per cent of my mental concentration. I was also using whatever problem-solving skills I have to realise that everything was going to fall to the floor and trying to work out how to momentarily suspend gravity to stop that from happening.

When Mark was showing us how to do it, he was using so little of his conscious brain that it was free to interact with us, allowing him to look from the barrel to his audience, explain what he was doing, crack jokes, and decide which of us was going to get the chance to have a go and show how hard it really was. Mark certainly wasn't worried about

---

[79]Frayling, 2017, p.61.
[80]Ibid. p.75.

dropping everything: he knew he wasn't going to, not just in his head, but in his hands. Just as his tools have been shaped by his grip, so the shape of his own hands takes a form he no longer has to think about, his grip on the staves moulded by years of repetition.

Whether you're making the construction of a wooden barrel look like a magic trick, or riding a bike or driving a car, when we learn how to do something well (or even badly) we no longer think about each individual action and step – many of them become routine. That's why someone like Gazza can mistake his remarkable skill for instinct – that's how it feels by the time you've practised so much that you're not even aware of exercising your talent. It's the same thing when musicians or writers feel like they're channelling some mysterious force from beyond themselves – the words and notes no longer feel like they're being generated by conscious thought. But conscious thought is where the skill originated: over time, and hours of practice, it starts to feel innate.

This is what George Sturt realised while he was trying to appear useful in his wheelwright's shop:

> The work was more of an art—a very fascinating art—than a science; and in this art, as I say, the brain had its share. A good wheelwright knew by art but not by reasoning the proportion to keep between spokes and felloes; and so too a good smith knew how tight a two-and-a-half inch tyre should be made for a five-foot wheel and how tight for a four-foot, and so on. He felt it, in his bones. It was a perception with him. But there was no science in it; no reasoning. Every detail stood by itself, and had to be learnt either by trial and error or by tradition.[81]

According to popular science, it takes 10,000 hours to perfect such skills. This general theory has been discredited by some researchers who have shown the amount varies by profession and discipline, but it refuses to go away, and it's

---

[81]Sturt, George, 1930, Chapter 1.

interesting to note that this seemingly immense amount of time just happens to work out at six hours a day, six days a week, for around five-and-a-half years – about the length of a traditional craftsperson's apprenticeship.

As basic skills become internalised, the parts of the brain devoted to learning can combine them to form higher skills, and apply them in different ways before moving on to learn the next new skill. When we become skilled at something, our brains resemble the technology tree in a computer game such as Sid Meier's *Civilization,* where you start off in ancient times learning basic technologies, and each one you learn unlocks the chance to learn the next, so over 20-odd hours of playing time, you go from inventing an alphabet to mastering interplanetary space travel. In *Civilization III* (my favourite iteration) it's good to start with an idea of how you intend to win – because there's more than one way. Let's say you decide from the offset that your strategy is to win a military victory by building tanks before anyone else does, and you plan your research accordingly. You unlock the capacity to build tanks by researching Motorized Transport. To research that, you need to already have researched Mass Production, and you can't get to that without both Combustion and Replaceable Parts. Combustion requires both Steel and Refining, both of which require the Corporation, which in turn requires Industrialization, and so on, all the way back to the wheel. You can't get to tanks without having first researched such technologies as Steam Power, Magnetism, Theology, Gunpowder, Map Making, and the Alphabet, each one of which was an absolute breakthrough, opening up new possibilities when you first reached it, every one long forgotten or taken for granted by the time you're building your first tank. And yes, you're damn right this is my idea of fun.

In this way, as we develop higher-level skills as individuals, we mirror the evolution of civilisation at large, each layer of ability built on top of the last, each newly-learned skill relying on old ones that have become routinised. This is the

119

interplay not just of hand and head, but of the various centres of memory and knowledge that move from one part of the brain to another as they become ingrained. As Sennett says, "In the higher stages of skill, there is a constant interplay between tacit knowledge and self-conscious awareness, the tacit knowledge serving as an anchor, the explicit awareness serving as critique and corrective".[82]

The reason it's important to dig so deep into the nature of skill and learning in this way is that once you appreciate it, it throws a harsh spotlight onto the sheer idiocy of modern industrial working practices. People are wired in such a way that they derive satisfaction, motivation and feelings of worth from a particular way of working. Managerial attempts to control workers and maximise their output invariably end up doing the direct opposite of what people need in order to feel fulfilled and worthwhile. That's why the concept of craft as defined by the Arts & Crafts movement has such unshakeable appeal. And that's why the philosophy of craft production enjoys a revival every time corporate working practices produce a dick move which they then try and sell as progress.

Taking it apart to see how it works

In *The Nature and Art of Workmanship* (2007) David Pye suggests that workmanship (or skill) can be broken down into a series of movements and conscious processes, just like Mass Production can be measured as the result of Industrialization, Combustion, Steam Power and so on. He distinguishes between two types of workmanship. First is the "workmanship of risk", where the final outcome is dependent to some degree on the skill and judgement of the maker, like the skill and judgement of a furniture maker in carving, turning and joining wood to create a new chair. The other type is "the workmanship of certainty", where the

---

[82]Sennett, 2009, p.50.

quality of the final product is assured before the worker even starts, thanks to the technology of mass production that – for example – allows millions of non-craftspeople to put together pre-cut parts to create millions of identical IKEA chairs, so long as they can handle odd tools and weird hieroglyphs. It's interesting that Pye phrases this comparison in terms of certainty and risk, because if there's one thing large corporations hate more than upstart craft producers, it's the concept of risk.

Corporations are obsessed with efficiency. The machines of the Industrial Revolution didn't just change the speed with which things could be done; they transformed the nature of how tasks could be performed. I promise this is the last time I'll squeeze in a reference to *Civilization III*, but the industrialised division of labour created a situation that, if it was replicated in the mechanics of the game, would mean you could have one person researching Industrialization, another researching Steam Power and another researching Combustion all at the same time, but each with no sense of how their work fitted onto the overall technology tree. Instead of researching Alphabet in order to get to Writing and from there to have the satisfaction of building a library, one person is just researching Alphabet over and over again, another person Pottery, their neighbour The Wheel, with no sense of completion. You could probably be building tanks by the Roman era, winning the game two thousand years ahead of schedule, but with no joy whatsoever in that accomplishment for any of the players who made it happen.

In its broadest form, the concept of division of labour goes back to the dawn of civilisation, and was first explored by the ancient Greeks. As soon as we began working together as tribes and then societies, with agriculture allowing a few people to grow food for a larger group rather than everyone hunting and gathering for themselves, people other than farmers were able to pursue and develop a range of different specialisms. When Plato puts forward the idea of the state in *The Republic*, he constructs it via division of labour,

121

proposing that "it will need a farmer, a builder, and a weaver, and also, I think, a shoemaker and one or two others to provide for our bodily needs. So that the minimum state would consist of four or five men".[83]

So the Industrial Revolution didn't create the division of labour, but it did exponentially multiply the *subdivisions* of it: Plato's shoemaker was replaced by a leather tanner, a cutter, a stitcher, a stapler, a hammerer of heels, and so on. The minimum size required for Plato's state grew exponentially, but the productivity of that state grew even more.

In 1812, Sir Richard Philips visited Marc Brunel's factory in Battersea, London, where shoes and boots were being made for the Duke of Wellington's army:

> [The process] is full of ingenuity, and, in regard to subdivision of labour, brings this fabric on a level with the oft-admired manufactory of pins. Every step in it is effected by the most elegant and precise machinery; while, as each operation is performed by one hand, so each shoe passes through twenty-five hands, who complete from the hide, as supplied by the currier, a hundred pairs of strong and well-finished shoes per day. All the details are performed by the ingenious application of the mechanic powers; and all the parts are characterised by precision, uniformity, and accuracy. As each man performs but one step in the process, which implies no knowledge of what is done by those who go before or follow him, so the persons employed are not shoemakers, but wounded soldiers, who are able to learn their respective duties in a few hours.[84]

The reference to pin-making is a call-back to a more famous description of the industrial division of labour. Adam Smith visited a pin factory to explore the subject for *Wealth of Nations*, and found himself torn. He calculated that ten men working in a pin factory with division of labour between separate tasks might contribute to a joint effort of 48,000

[83]Plato, *The Republic*, (Penguin Classics edition, London, 2012) p.103.
[84]Philips, Richard, A Morning's Walk from London to Kew, 1817, quoted on Wikipedia https://en.wikipedia.org/wiki/Shoemaking

pins per day – 4,800 per man. But each man working alone would struggle to make twenty.

The cost of this is that these men find themselves deskilled, their spirits dulled. Smith saw the industrialised division of labour as the source of the wealth of nations, but the cost of that would be "the almost entire corruption and degeneracy of the great body of the people... unless the government takes some pains to prevent it".[85] Government, of course, did not.

This is why the shoemaking example is worth quoting at length. If we look at it from the point of view of the nation as a whole, the benefit is undeniable: not only are more shoes being made more cheaply; they can now be made by unskilled, wounded soldiers who would otherwise likely be begging on the streets. The downsides are at an individual level: there's no work for the skilled shoemaker, no job satisfaction or fulfilment for the wounded soldier, and no chance of customising the design of the shoe to meet the tastes of the individual customer.

But ever since ancient Greece, the welfare of society as a whole has outweighed the welfare of the individual within it. For most of human history, we have been expected to be prepared to die for our king, country or god, so working in a boring job in a factory might seem like a relatively small sacrifice for the greater good, especially when you get paid enough at the end of the week to be able to buy a spare box of pins or even a decent pair of shoes.

The Arts & Crafts movement could never hope to turn the tide of industrialisation: placing the needs of a few skilled individuals above the needs of the nation as a whole was simply never going to work. Over the course of the movement's existence, work became *more* sub-divided, not

---

[85] Smith, Adam, *An Inquiry into the Nature and Causes of the Wealth of Nations* (London, 1776) Book V, Chapter 1, Part III, Article II

less, thanks to the increasing belief that science, rather than art or craft, should be the driving force behind the means of production, and that the deskilling, terminal boredom and loss of dignity of the individual worker was a small price to pay for the prosperity of society as a whole.

This philosophy reached its apex in the doctrine of scientific management, a term coined by Frederick Winslow Taylor. Taylor worked in a steel factory and shared Henry "you can have the car in any colour so long as it's black" Ford's obsession with breaking a job down into its simplest steps, so that pretty much anyone could be taught to do one step repetitively. He was obsessed with the idea of efficiency, introducing his 1911 book, *The Principles of Scientific Management*, by quoting President Roosevelt saying, "The conservation of our national resources is only preliminary to the larger question of national efficiency," and offering his book as the remedy. He pointed out "the great loss which the whole country is suffering through inefficiency in almost all of our daily acts," and proposed that "the remedy for this inefficiency lies in systematic management". [86] Taylor introduced time and motion studies, using a stopwatch to time workers performing tasks, with the aim of finding the single most efficient way of getting each scientifically sub-divided task completed.

The principles of Taylorism and Fordism would dominate organisational theory and behaviour for more than half a century, and they still retain huge power today. Commercial organisations hate both inefficiency and risk. Faced with a choice between a risky strategy that might well boost income, or a certain strategy that is sure to reduce costs, western business management is trained always to choose the latter.

The last advertising campaign I ever worked on was for a

---

[86]Taylor, Frederick Winslow, *The Principles of Scientific Management* (1911) accessed via www.gutenberg.org.

dairy brand where we had an idea that we thought might appeal to a large number of people and change how they thought about choosing which brand of butter they wanted to buy. We couldn't guarantee that it would definitely work because people are weird and unpredictable, and don't always do what they say they're going to do. So we did some research about the ad with our target audience. It was broadly positive, but there were still a few questions, so we tweaked the ad and researched it again. This is normal practice in advertising. But on this occasion, the client was so nervous of failure – not because of the welfare of the brand but because their line manager was a bit scary – that we refined and researched so often that in the end the client spent the entire media budget for the ad on research instead: we reached a point where we knew it would definitely work, but there was no money left to run it. The client genuinely thought they had done a good job by minimising the risk of the ad not motivating people to buy their butter, rather than a bad job of getting to a situation where they couldn't actually show it to anyone who might be thinking about buying butter.

Anyone who has worked in advertising research has a similar story. Advertising is fascinating, because it's where the theory of marketing meets the reality of people, and when that happens, science often goes out of the window. Almost daily when I worked in advertising, I'd remember my A-level economics lessons and the first assumptions that models of supply and demand make: one, that people have perfect knowledge of the market; and two, that people will behave in a perfectly rational way when making purchasing decisions. Advertising helps destroy the former, and proves the latter to be wishful thinking on a par with believing in Santa Claus or Donald Trump's hair.

Even when business management theory accepts that, as people, we might behave irrationally in our role as consumers, it still largely maintains a belief that in organisations and in our jobs, we behave rationally. Even if

125

we did – which we don't – this displays a poor understanding of what rationality means. It ignores the uncomfortable relationship between IQ and emotional intelligence. The former is neat and measurable; the latter is messy and unpredictable – especially if you have no idea what it is. The problem with scientific management and the structures and processes it created are that it attempts to understand people solely in rational terms, when people are anything but.

When you simplify a task to the point where it is so mindless that a machine could do it, you are treating a person as if they were a machine. You are separating their skill – however basic it is – from both knowledge and agency. Around the time of the Great Exhibition in 1851 – which to the future members of the Arts & Crafts movement represented everything that was wrong about where the world was going – Ruskin railed against the "degradation of the operative into a machine, which, more than any other evil of the times, is leading the mass of nations everywhere into vain, incoherent, destructive struggling for freedom." He urged people to appreciate that the worker was not "activated by steam, magnetism, gravitation, or any other agent of calculable force" but by his "soul".[87]

Protests like this always sound idealistic to cynical managers who are tasked with focusing on profit rather than the welfare of their workers' souls. But if you are performing repetitive actions with little or no say in how you do your job and with no meaningful conception of how your labour contributes to the finished whole, it leads to more than just boredom: lack of motivation, job dissatisfaction, higher staff turnover, lack of teamwork, and deep divisions between workers and management all become endemic.

This doesn't mean tools and machines are intrinsically bad.

---

[87]Ruskin quoted in Langlands, 2017, p.33

It just means we should think more carefully about what they do and how they are used. Some machines in factories saved workers from unpleasant or boring jobs. Others did work that people hadn't been able to do before, because the machines were stronger or moved in ways the human body couldn't. Machines don't tire physically, and can perform jobs to a greater standard of accuracy and consistency.

Many machines were actually welcomed by the workers who had to use them. If you no longer have to haul sacks of grain to the top of the brewery or dig out a mash tun by hand, you have more time to do something more creative. The issue with machines for the craftsperson is when they allow tasks to be broken down to such an extent that you no longer have any overall conception of the brewing of a batch of beer, and no say in how that process goes outside your tiny part of it.

Scientific management is obsessed with measurement, and even though many aspects of it have been discredited or are no longer relevant, measurement has only become more important to business today, and beyond that, to every aspect of our lives. Album and film reviews have been reduced to ratings out of five stars. We are asked to evaluate and rate every single thing we buy online and every interaction with sales and call centre staff. In doing so, we end up losing important information and insight.

If you've ever filled out a feedback survey and become frustrated that it's asking you repeatedly about how quickly the product was delivered or how nice the packaging was, and all you want to tell them is that none of this matters because the damned thing didn't actually work but the fucking form never gives you the opportunity to say that, you've got a head start on understanding the problems and limitations of scientific management. It measures what it thinks is important to measure, and ignores anything that can't be measured in a mechanistic way.

Even in the most sub-divided production line process, there are breakdowns, environmental factors and inconsistencies that require human inventiveness and creativity to sort out. Sennett argues that "Highly specialised skills represent not just a laundry list of procedures but a culture formed around these actions," and gives the example of steelworkers in 1900 who had to develop a set of customs, signs and understandings to allow them to work together safely in an environment where they couldn't hear each other, and only see each other poorly.[88]

George Sturt gives another insight into the issue by exploring the difference between manufacture, customisation and repair:

> A machine could turn out a wheel—of sorts—but to mend one required, in many cases, long experience... at repairs [an apprentice] found out what was needful for the current day; what this road required, and that hill; what would satisfy Farmer So-and-So's temper, or suit his pocket; what the farmer's carter favoured or his team wanted... It wasn't quite enough to know how to do this or that; you needed also to know something about why... The machines are tireless; they can do heavier and quicker work than men, but they cannot originate; they can merely reproduce what craftsmen set them to do.[89]

These cultural and contextual aspects exist in any industrialised workplace and cannot be measured by time and motion studies. They are essential not just for the individual worker, but for the smooth running of the workplace as a whole. Richard Sennett jumps into this in great detail in *The Craftsman*, carefully building an argument that craft skills and a culture that seeks to preserve the link between hand and head has advantages way beyond anything Taylor could measure. He points out that today, organisations from call centres to the NHS are still trying to measure their output and success in numerical targets. This creates a conflict between doing a good job and following

---

[88]Sennett, 2009, pp.106-107
[89]Sturt, George, 1930, Chapter 17.

the correct procedure – which should surely be the same thing. But when an NHS worker attempts a workaround learned from practical experience that results in someone living instead of dying, they can still be criticised if they didn't follow the correct procedure in doing so. A call centre worker often faces the impossible choice between delighting a customer and getting a maximum feedback score from them, and finishing the call within the target time period, when their performance is evaluated on both scores.

As societies, our underlying acquiescence to the ideas that hand and head are separate, and that head work is superior to handwork, have set us on a path where we value whatever we can measure, delineate and define intellectually, and devalue what we cannot. Sennett points out that on intelligence tests such as Stanford-Binet, we are evaluated on whether or not we get the correct answer to the question or not within a certain timeframe. Such tests penalise those who take the time to reflect.

There aren't just different kinds of knowledge – there's been a long, steady drift from one kind to the other. In the name of efficiency, we have devalued innate know-how and idolised learned, quantifiable knowledge simply because it is measurable. By doing so, we lose sight of valuable learnings, skills and insight, and end up in a situation where doing what is right can be different from doing what is correct. No wonder the maverick cop who breaks the rules but gets the job done is such a powerful and appealing trope in Hollywood movies and TV shows.

We're starting to see now that, while it's great to have the option to buy crafted rather than industrial products, the deep attraction we have to craft has more to do with the satisfaction we get from whatever job we do, and the processes and systems that constrain us within that. In the previous chapter, we showed that Arts & Crafts, while it failed to change the mainstream direction of work, lived on as counter-cultural ideal to the system it failed to displace. In this chapter, we've explored the concepts of division of labour and scientific management and shown that even though they are severely flawed, they still retain a massive influence over how our work is organised, and how we react to that. People are messy and complicated in every aspect of their lives. We're not robots. If we look at science, art and craft as different ways of approaching and making sense of the world, we can see that the scientific method of observing, recording and analysing – while being essential to our sense of progress – gives an incomplete picture of who we are and what makes us tick.

In short – whenever industrial capitalism gets too scientific and regulatory on our asses, we seek an alternative point of view through which to vent our frustration. Every time work tries to view us as less than human, we counter that by rediscovering the counter-cultural ideals of craft. Established in the nineteenth century, it has repeated itself since then, returning to rescue us whenever the cold logic of efficiency and profit above all else threatens to dehumanise us.

Chapter 6:
The secret tyranny of the round window

The world of new and improved

The doctrine of scientific management peaked around the 1970s. In 1970, 25% of American workers were employed in industrial manufacturing, compared with 10% today.[90] That same decade, the figure was closer to 30% in the UK.[91] By this time, we'd had decades of time and motion studies, and generations of the same families following each other into factories to work on production lines. When I was small, we used to watch a programme called *Play School*, the mention of which can still moisten the eyes of any Brit over the age of 40. One of the best bits of *Play School* was when we all got to look through one of the magic windows. On one shaky studio set wall sat a square window, a round window and an arched window. The first thrill was guessing which window we'd be looking through today, a choice the presenter would draw out for what seemed to be an agonising eternity as the national's pre-school kids yelled "SQUARE! NO, ROUND. ROOOUUUND!"

Once we were through the window and out of our misery, we were watching a short piece of film about stuff that grown-ups did in the real, grown-up world. And in my memory, at least half the time, what we got to watch was

[90]https://www.economist.com/finance-and-economics/2005/09/29/industrial-metamorphosis
[91]https://www.ons.gov.uk/economy/nationalaccounts/uksectoraccounts/compendium/economicreview/april2019/longtermtrendsinukemployment1861to2018

stuff being made on a production line. We'd see components being handled by men in brown overalls or women in white coats and hair nets, and after all the excitement of guessing which window we were getting, the follow-up thrill was being the first to guess what object we were witnessing being made.

"It's toy cars. Look, that woman's putting a wheel on."

"No it's not, it's as clock, that's clockwork!"

"Oh, hang on – it's a TELLYPHONE!"

It was the best bit of the programme, a relief from the hippyish studio presenters whose manner of talking to small children made them seem not so much stoned as concussed. *Play School* fetishized the production line, and made working on one look like the coolest thing ever. Looking back, it's clear that a generation of kids was being primed for a lifetime of low-skilled manual labour. It strikes me now as being little different from the ideological indoctrination we'd more readily associate with North Korea or Soviet Russia, but it was done by the BBC, so it was subtler and nicer.

The years following the Moon landings were a futuristic decade where every other TV programme speculated about what we would be doing "by the year 2000". Every week, ten million Brits watched the TV programme *Tomorrow's World*, which painted a rosy future that was all about technological innovations such as digital watches, pocket calculators and mobile phones, and never touched on what the societal or cultural impact of "progress" might be.

Everything was supersonic, streamlined and modernised. Supermarkets replaced independent grocers and butchers, bread became Wonderbread in the States and Mother's Pride in the UK, ham became Spam, and anything powdered and instant was seen as an exciting new innovation. The future was plastic, processed, and uniform, just like the cheese we now bought in jars or cellophane packets. It was when we stopped looking for things that were nicer than they absolutely had to be.

We were so enthralled by the principle, by the *rightness* of technological advancement, that we rarely stopped to question if we actually wanted it in the first place. Division of labour became so efficient that we were now making more stuff than we actually needed. Manufacturers created electric carving knives, toothbrushes and can openers because they could, not because consumers were demanding them. For the first time in history, the average working- or lower-middle-class person had enough stuff, but manufacturers had to keep on selling us *more* stuff because they would collapse if they didn't. And if everything was cheap and everything was the same, without the possibility of the craftperson's customisation and personalisation, they had to convince us that we had to buy this new thing because it was what everyone wanted, even though sometimes the only people who did want it were the people making it. We were taught that valuable objects were disposable and replaceable rather than repairable, and became accustomed to the concept of planned obsolescence and eternal upgrades. The idea of progress, as defined by the unstoppable, Terminator-esque logic of eternal consumption and constant purchasing, became its own prison.

The call of the past

In October 1973, an interesting new dynamic was thrown into the mix. As a protest against the West's support for Israel, the Arab states quadrupled the price of oil, announcing that "the era of cheap energy is over." Recession and energy blackouts created a weird sense of being capable of having anything we had ever wanted while being keenly aware that, at the same time, we might lose it all. The notion of inevitable progress came into question,

133

and science fiction developed a darker, dystopian streak, asking the questions that *Tomorrow's World* didn't, about where all this was taking us. If the enemy in 1950s Sci-Fi was the Red Menace of Soviet Russia thinly disguised as Martians, the future nemesis of the 1970s – as expressed in movies from *A Clockwork Orange* to *Logan's Run* and in punky, in-yer-face comics such as *2000AD* – was increasingly ourselves.

When the present is scary and the future uncertain, we escape to the past. People began harking back to the Victorian and Edwardian era, repeating the echo of that age's own conflict between progress and nostalgia for a semi-mythical lost past. We started to look for frills and filigree to contrast with streamlined modernism. Laura Ashley sought out Victorian designs to clothe fashionable women in floor-length dresses that, at the time, were as confrontational as the mini-skirt had been a decade before. Sanderson sold William Morris's designs on coordinating fabrics and wallpapers to thousands of homes. *The Country Diary of an Edwardian Lady*, first written in 1906 by Edith Holden, was published in 1977 – 57 years after her untimely death – and stayed in the *Sunday Times* bestseller list for a record 63 weeks, becoming the best-selling book of the 1970s in the UK. In an age of consumerist excess, the homespun, stripped-back country look was suddenly cool. Kitchens were farmhouse style, pine was stripped, and the new Range Rover in the drive allowed you to pretend you were off to pick up your food from the farm rather than the supermarket. *The Good Life* – a sitcom in which a suburban couple attempt to become self-sufficient – ran from 1975 to 1978 and was one of the most popular TV shows of the decade in the UK, and was also shown in the United States, Canada, Australia, South Africa and, naturally, Belgium.

All of this was seasoned by a good dollop of hippie idealism. People who came of age in the 1970s often say that, for most people, the '70s is when the '60s really happened. Peter Korn, who began his career as a furniture maker at the time, writes that in America, "despite every sign of worldly success, adult life looked shallow and, in the twin shadows of Vietnam and the civil rights movement, morally bankrupt."[92]

Bearing this in mind, it's no coincidence that the American craft beer movement began on the west coast, and it's certainly no surprise that it eventually settled on craft beer as a name. Ken Grossman's first business was a homebrew equipment shop, supporting a hobby he pursued alongside "other homesteading activities that included raising goats and making cheese", a lifestyle that echoes *The Good Life*.[93] Craft, in turning away from the mainstream sense of linear progress, is inherently counter-cultural. And in the UK, the first place where this general, widespread sense of dissatisfaction coalesced into an active movement of resistance was in the pub.

When CAMRA formed in 1971, it started as a small movement. But it tapped into something many were feeling. In 1973, an elderly, cantankerous and much-loved Scottish TV presenter called Fyfe Robertson went in search of the perfect pint. A recent BBC2 documentary, *The Home That 2 Built*, shows footage of him visiting a modern, automated brewery. Even before we get to the beer it brews, we can see him looking aghast at the way it is made, as he says in voice-over:

> Here electronics reduce an ancient and earthy craft to flashing lights and twiddled knobs. Eight different twiddles create eight different beers. You can smell them – just – but you can't see a drop, everything hidden behind austere, immaculate steel.[94]

Later in the programme, "Robbie" questions a CAMRA activist on what is different about "proper" beer, and

[92]Korn, 2017, p.19.
[93]Quoted in Acitelli, 2013, p.34.
[94]The Home That 2 Built, BBC iPlayer:
https://www.bbc.co.uk/programmes/b04pmw33

initially he's unable to articulate it, just that it's proper, traditional British beer that has been made the right way, nothing like the dreaded "keg." Looking back forty years later, *The Home That 2 Built* describes CAMRA as "the first campaigning group of the '70s to fight back against the corporations and supermarkets that were sweeping all before them".

This distaste for what corporations were doing to us as consumers was inflamed by what they were doing to us as workers. The logical progression of division of labour, where the worker is treated like a machine, is that eventually the worker can be replaced by a machine altogether.

In 1979, film director Hugh Hudson shot a commercial written by adman and soon-to-become-another-film-director Paul Weiland, for the launch of the Fiat Strada. The commercial made history by being two minutes long and taking up the entire centre break of *News at Ten* at a time when Britain had three TV channels, only one of them commercial. Hailed by many industry pundits as the best TV ad ever made, it takes the idea of the modern production line and makes it cinematic, even artistic. Unless you squint through the windows of the cars at the end, no human being appears in the ad: instead, angular robots glide across the factory floor, assembling the cars that will eventually speed around a test track. Rather than employ the futuristic music of, say, Kraftwerk to soundtrack these scenes, the rousing "Figaro's Aria" from Gioachino Rossini's opera *The Barber of Seville* is used to create a juxtaposition between what looked to most viewers at the time like science fiction, and a sense of continuity and Italian tradition. What the viewers at the time didn't know is that when Hugh Hudson's production team arrived at the Fiat factory in Turin to shoot the ad, they had to run a gauntlet of pickets and burning tyres lit by workers protesting about robots taking their jobs.

As well as encapsulating the tensions that "progress"

created through the 1970s, the commercial also manages to illustrate another conflict that began then and still rumbles today.

Arguably the biggest problems modern-day beer-lovers have with the concept of craft beer is that it has been appropriated by the marketers of big breweries and is therefore "meaningless". While I disagree, I still can't help eye-rolling every time I spot the word "crafted" appearing on the packaging of mass-produced industrial beers. It's so obvious. It's so *lame*. And it has the opposite effect of what they hope to achieve: the people who market brands such as Foster's know they would be laughed at if they tried to call it a craft beer, so they write something like "crafted to refresh" on the side of the can, hoping that consumers will make a subliminal association between a cheap lager and more aspirational craft beer. Instead, they come across as cynical and heartless, desperately stealing something that doesn't belong to them, and wearing it like a dress or suit that's two sizes too small, unaware of how ridiculous they look.

Wherever you stand on the issue of the language and imagery of craft beer being appropriated by the very corporations craft rose against, this is not a new phenomenon. The strapline at the end of the 1979 Fiat Strada ad was "Hand-built by robots".

On one level, this is the kind of gentle joke British advertising used to excel at – *because the robots didn't have any hands!* On another level, it's the kind of Jedi mind-trick British advertising also used to excel at because it borrows reassuring language to normalise something new and possibly scary. It provides the perfect illustration of the tension between living in a time of enormous technological change and at least partially wanting to hark back to simpler days.

"When advertising people use 'crafted' as a substitute for

'manufactured', they are attempting to delude the public into believing that something has been made by hand in a carefully old-fashioned way," says Christopher Frayling when he mentions the ad in his 1982 essay on what makes a skill:

> ...the reassuring connotations of 'hand-built' and 'craft' are calculated to offset the less reassuring connotations of robots and space-age technology. Craft is trustworthy, microchips are not – at least, not yet. It is as if the advertisers are selling our own nostalgia back to us at a profit... Advertisers can rely on the simple word 'crafted' to relieve for a moment the complex anxieties which these social and economic processes have created.[95]

"Crafted" according to Frayling, is one of those words that "beguile as well as inform", and it has been for at least forty years. Rather than being a problem specific to the craft beer world, it happens with any product, in any market, whenever the desire for something more – *ahem* – crafted becomes too big to ignore. We want to hear it. We are reassured by it. It's a mental balm. We like to and want to believe that products are made by hand, which makes it easier for unscrupulous manufacturers to convince us that their products are.

So why do we find the idea of "hand-made" products so appealing? For the same reason we liked the idea of Merrie England in the 1880s and the *Diary of an Edwardian Country Lady* in the 1970s, and why so many people still watch *Friends* today.

Nostalgia ain't what it used to be

Nostalgia – from the Greek *nóstos*, meaning "returning home", and *álgos*, meaning "pain" or "ache", was originally diagnosed as a disease affecting Swiss mercenaries who pined for their mountainous homeland while fighting in

---

[95]Frayling, 2017, p.61.

France and Italy in the seventeenth century. It was considered a serious ailment, to the extent that people were recorded as dying from it. It wasn't until the 1920s that the word took on its modern usage. Nostalgia – like craft itself – is a product of industrialization and progress, in this case given a big boost by the First World War's demonstration of just how thrilling industrialization and progress could be.

The way we have warped nostalgia from meaning homesickness to a longing for the past speaks volumes. Svetlana Boym, in *The Future of Nostalgia* (2001), argues that this happened because the Industrial Revolution changed not just our relationship with time, but our very conception of it:

> From the seventeenth century to the nineteenth century, the representation of time itself changed; it moved away from allegorical human figures – an old man, a blind youth holding an hourglass, a woman with bared breasts representing Fate – to the impersonal language of numbers: railroad schedules, the bottom line of industrial progress. Time was no longer shifting sand: time was money.[96]

Boym points out that even the word "revolution" suggests a cyclical conception of time. Work was once governed by the passing of the seasons. Clock faces were round and the hands travelled in perpetual circles. The world spins and comes back round again, on its elliptical path around the sun. In 1927 – just as the modern conception of nostalgia was taking root – astrophysicist Arthur Eddington proposed instead the concept of "Time's Arrow", that time is in fact linear, constant and irreversible.

We have now become disconnected from time as we experienced it until the last couple of centuries. We may not conceptualise it in these terms, but if progress relentlessly follows time's arrow, then if you don't want to move

---

[96]Boym, Svetlana, *The Future of Nostalgia* (Basic Books, New York, 2001) p.9.

forward with it, the yearning, the ache, to move backward or even stand still must necessarily grow in relation to the speed of forward movement. The past feels like home, and we grow sick with longing for it.

Nostalgia is sentimental, but we shouldn't beat ourselves up too much for (mis-)remembering or re-imagining the past in warm, glowing hues. As individuals, we're conditioned to remember our own pleasant memories more vividly then the boring or terrible ones – I can remember my wedding day in 2002 better than I can remember last Wednesday. We constantly re-evaluate our own pasts. Kids at school who took the piss out of me for loving Big Country or even beat me up for liking The Smiths would, when we met at weddings ten or twenty years later, talk about how we all loved playing them together in the common room. For my part, Friday nights on BBC4 have almost convinced me that, at the same time, I actually liked Duran Duran. As socio-political groups, we compound our mis-rememberings, especially when we weren't there to begin with. People like me imagine the 1960s as a time of freedom and extraordinary creativity when I would have been happier than I am today. Others, somewhat to the right of me on the political spectrum, would prefer to take society back to the 1950s, when everything was proper and orderly and decent. We are both equally deluded.

The words "craft" and "crafted" work partly because nostalgia is so strong in us. Crafts are skills that have been developed over time and take more time to learn well. They represent continuity and stability, a slower pace of life than we enjoy now, and a life that is more connected to everything around it. These are the virtues of craft, but also the dangers of it.

Frayling talks about the long-running campaign for Hovis bread in the UK. This was so popular in my childhood that it was a meme decades before that term entered popular use. It was repeated and parodied and adapted for years, and occasionally still is, almost fifty years after it first aired. The visual is of a young boy in a flat cap pushing his bike up a steep hill to visit the baker for a loaf of bread. The accompanying audio is an old man narrating his childhood experience. If you've never seen it, the best way I can give you an idea of how effective it was is to say that it launched the career of an ambitious young adman called Ridley Scott.

Hovis was, and still is, made in a massive factory where taste comes well down a list of quality criteria including appearance and cost. If you compare Hovis to freshly-baked bread, it doesn't actually have the taste or texture of bread at all. I make bread with flour, water, yeast and salt. Hovis makes its "Tasty Medium Sliced Wholemeal Bread" with "Wholemeal Flour (Wheat), Water, Yeast, Caramelised Sugar, Wheat Protein, Wheat Flour (with added Calcium, Iron, Niacin, Thiamin), Salt, Soya Flour, Vegetable Oil (Palm, Rapeseed), Preservative: E282, Emulsifiers: E471, E472e, Flour Treatment Agent: Ascorbic Acid," and despite all those additives and preservatives, it still goes mouldy quicker than mine. So it's no surprise that Hovis and its competitors want to convince you that it is, in the words of that famous ad's strapline, "As good today as it's always been".

Frayling cites the Hovis ad as another example of adverts that "beguile as well as inform", cloaking a modern industrial product in crafted, pseudo-authentic imagery. It's as much of an issue in bread as it is in beer. But the existence of this war of deception leads us to a deeper point: our connection to the past is an idealised one, our vision blurred by nostalgia, like the Vaseline-smeared lens on a 1940s starlet. As Frayling, observes, "The history which underpins much of the 'craft revival' is, in fact, nostalgia masquerading as history".[97]

The fact is, for all its many faults, a modern loaf of

---

[97]Frayling, 2017, p.66.

industrial bread probably tastes better and is better for you than the bread of yesteryear. Wheat was often scarce, and bulked out with barley, oats, or rye flour. During the First World War – roughly around the time the Hovis ad was set – people were encouraged to make their own bread by mixing flour with pre-cooked rice, sago or potatoes, as well as haricot beans or barley, to make the flour go further. If bread was made with old flour, the degradation of the oils in the flour gave it a rancid taste. Before that, in the 18th and 19th centuries, unscrupulous bakers added alum, lime, chalk and even powdered bones to give bread the white appearance their customers favoured. Eating mouldy bread – sometimes the only choice other than starvation – ran the risk of contracting painful toxic diseases. As good today as it's always been? Hovis was selling itself short.

Similarly, for most of human history, people would have loved the quality and consistency in the beers we now take for granted. They may be bland and boring, but they're widely available and of consistent quality. The 1820 study *A Treatise on Adulterations of Food* revealed that, due to the high price of malt and hops, brewers and publicans would add wood shavings to beer to create bitterness, and "vitriol" (iron sulphate), alum and salt to create a decent head. When CAMRA activists talk about cask ale being "beer as it has always been brewed," they're actually talking about a way of making and dispensing beer that dates back only to the 1870s, when "running beers" were developed by the largest corporate brewers of the day to be brewed and sold quickly rather than undergoing long periods of storage, using the very latest scientific knowledge about fermentation.

The capacity to be bored by the bland consistency of Budweiser or Castlemaine XXXX is a luxury that was unavailable anywhere until 150 years ago, and when you travel to some developing countries, you quickly realise it remains so today for many of the world's beer drinkers.

Objectively, the mainstream in any market has raised

142

standards for most people. The big difference between the Arts & Crafts era and the modern world from the 1970s onwards is that Morris and his friends wanted to democratise beauty in an age when most people had very little, and ended up selling to a moneyed elite. Now, if you've got the money, you can still choose to buy expensive, crafted products. But if you don't want to, or can't afford to, there's a bewildering choice of perfectly adequate, if uninspiring, industrially-produced alternatives that you can probably afford. It may not be beautiful, but in the end, it was the mass production built on division of labour that democratised – if not beauty – at least some sense of comfort and pleasure. In the UK, an IKEA Ivar chair costs the equivalent of just two hours of your labour if you're earning the national legal minimum wage. (Plus another two hours of your labour to put the bastard together of course.)

The Outsider and the Bourgeois

The dull, stolid availability of mass-produced, commoditised goods provides the bedrock against which craft can take off and provide an alternative. In this aspect, it echoes the work of Colin Wilson, whose 1956 book *The Outsider* explores why artists and other creative people feel alienated from mainstream society.

Wilson suggested that there are basically two types of people: the Outsider and the Bourgeois. The Outsider finds the mainstream dull and boring, its attitudes complacent. The Outsider can't bear the idea of a normal dull, grey existence, So they hide in garrets and write poetry or existential novels, create art, or try, and go mad or kill themselves. Two of Wilson's case study outsiders are Vincent Van Gogh and T. E. Lawrence, and he builds a compelling thesis by exploring their lives and work.

The Bourgeois is, of course, a regular person who regards the Outsider as a bit weird. The Bourgeois is careful, conservative and conventional, proud of his lawn, his beautiful wife and his adorable children, and his abs, because, hey, he likes an occasional beer with the guys– who doesn't? – but he makes sure he keeps in shape by going to the gym, and while he might have been a bit wild at university, it was what was expected of you then, you were only young! But when you graduate, it's time to calm down, to knuckle down, to settle down, to Choose Life, to find out where things are in B&Q, to buy soup in cartons instead of tins, to get a German shepherd dog called Prince, and to build for your future and then, Jesus willing, build for your kid's future.

Oh, just fucking kill me right now. You're with me on this, aren't you? You've read this far – we should all want to be the Outsiders, right?

Well… no. Wilson's brilliant insight is that the Outsider and the Bourgeois enjoy a symbiotic relationship – they need each other to survive. Without the Bourgeois working on farms and in factories and shops, the Outsider would starve. Without the Bourgeois working in humdrum jobs providing utilities, the Outsider wouldn't have water in the taps or light to work by in their garret. Without the Bourgeois working in offices and call centres and council chambers, the Outsider wouldn't have the infrastructure that allows them the freedom to sit in comfort and safety and dream of better things. The Outsider is completely reliant upon the Bourgeois they look down on.

But contrary to some branches of political thought, the Outsider isn't just some rebel without a cause, sponging off the system instead of getting a proper job. Left to themselves, the Bourgeois would stagnate. By thinking outside the system and seeing things in a different way, Wilson argues that the Outsider gives society the ideas that create forward motion and help it progress. Without the Outsider provoking, questioning, resisting, agitating and inspiring, Bourgeois society would gather dust, and eventually just grind to a halt, without anyone really noticing. The two sides are two halves of a system that provides security and stability on one side, and inspiration and progress on the other.

People who love the idea of craft as a counter-cultural movement are completely reliant on the stability and the products of the mainstream. The truth is, it's a luxury to be able to give up your job in finance, IT or selling cardboard packaging, swap the suit for a pair of overalls and start mashing in.

Why did the modern craft beer movement begin in the richest country in the world, and then spread to other affluent countries first? Because craft is elitist. It's a luxury. It always was, even in the Arts & Crafts days. But now, there's a stable, bland, conformist alternative to set yourself against. And that's *fine*: it doesn't mean craft is fake or false. It's a vital part of the system, even if it does produce some odd quirks. The counter-culture of craft toys with the mainstream, challenges convention and appropriates useful bits as its own. When everyone can afford an IKEA chair, craft gives us quirky chairs in garish fabrics, or the means to customise the IKEA chair and make it our own. When science gives us malting barley strains with a higher yield than ever before, we revive heritage varieties like Chevallier. When science gives us laboratory-cultivated yeast strains that give brewers greater control over the consistency of flavour and character in their beers, brewers become fascinated with wild yeast strains and develop a deeper understanding of them using techniques that had been originally developed in the labs where single strains were cultivated.

In return, the Outsiders of craft are changing the Bourgeois of the mainstream. When I worked for Whitbread's advertising agency making ads for Stella Artois and Heineken, most of my clients were career marketers with little regard for beer. Many of the people responsible for selling those beers in the UK couldn't have told you the ingredients of beer or the history of the brewery. Some of them never drank beer themselves. Their previous jobs may have been on pet food or laundry detergent. They'd stick around for eighteen months or two years, then they'd be off to a more senior role on cola or processed cheese. Now, when I meet people working in similar roles for brands like Guinness or Carlsberg, they tend to be passionate fans of craft beer themselves, learning the ropes as part of a career plan that is rooted long-term in beer, perhaps even leading towards starting a craft brewery of their own some day.

Playing among the ruins

Craft beer follows the broader field of arts and crafts in challenging mainstream conformity, modern efficiency, and things being no nicer than they have to be. But in one key respect, it's out of time with most other iterations of craft.

Returning to Christopher Frayling's argument about the deception of "crafted" products, he points out that things which are "crafted" or "hand-made" – genuinely or not – often come adorned in rural imagery. As Frayling argues, this is often used to disguise the industrial reality. Bread made in super-modern factories dresses up in rustic Edwardian clothes. Packaging for big dairy brands will often feature engraved illustrations of farmhouses. Pasta sauces have ads depicting an idyllic Italian country kitchen to sell products made in a factory in Kings Lynn.

Modern craft beer forms an interesting exception to this rule. It certainly began by evoking the same nostalgic, homespun rural imagery that characterised craft more broadly in the 1970s. For its logo, CAMRA adopted the image of a pewter tankard – a drinking vessel that was last in widespread use in the mid-nineteenth century. The labels of early American craft beers such as Anchor, Sierra Nevada, Samuel Adams and New Albion without exception featured hand-drawn, folksy illustrations of sailing ships, lakes, old-timey fellows hoisting CAMRA-style tankards, and – more

146

than anything else – dreamy mountain ranges.

But behind this imagery, craft beer was always more urban than rural. Goose Island – which for me always evoked a misty lake with a mountain backdrop – was actually named after a district in downtown Chicago that was once so industrialised it was nicknamed Little Hell. Like many early craft breweries, it was founded in a post-industrial space: Clybourn Avenue had once been home to thirty factories employing two thousand workers, and the brewery was previously a Turtle Wax factory. In his foreword to Steve Hindy's book *The Craft Beer Revolution*, John Hickenlooper, founder of the Wynkoop Brewery in Denver, writes about signing a lease for an abandoned warehouse in an old industrial district where the rent was a dollar per square foot per year. "We were… the first restaurant to open in LoDo [Lower Downtown] in five years," he writes. "Like Steve's business [Brooklyn Brewery] half a continent away and dozens of other around the country, we tried to build relationships with our neighbors, and through those relationships, rebuild neighborhoods".[98]

This trend has persisted into modern-day craft beer around the globe. In British cities, the railway arch is the spiritual home of the start-up craft brewery. In 2019, while I was in Australia giving the keynote speech at a craft beer conference, I hooked up with a couple of old work friends I hadn't seen since they'd emigrated over a decade before. When Sue and I worked together in London in the early noughties, we drank Sauvignon Blanc as if it were a religious calling. When she picked me up from the commuter train stop half an hour outside Melbourne's Central Business District, she said, "When we knew you were coming, we did some research to see if we were close to any craft brewery places. It turns out there are two of them very close to our house! But they both seem to be in units on *industrial estates*.

---

[98]Hindy, Steve, *The Craft Beer Revolution*, (Palgrave Macmillan, New York, 2014)

That can't be right, can it?" She trusted her satnav more than she trusted me, so Sue, her husband Steve and I ended up spending a wonderful afternoon exploring the sensory delights of Kiwi and Tasmanian hops. But I completely failed at the time to successfully articulate why Melbourne's hipsters were spending their Saturday afternoons hanging out next door to deserted suburban light industrial machinery manufacturers instead of in the city's vibrant, multi-cultural core or out at the beach.

Early craft brewers repurposed industrial equipment to jerry-build their breweries. The beer styles that have shaped craft beer – particularly porter and IPA – are themselves direct creations of the Industrial Revolution that the Arts & Crafts movement stood against, both in terms of the technology and scale of their production, and the newly urbanised mass populations of factory-, forge- and mill-workers who consumed them in record quantities.

In bars and taprooms, exposed heating ducts and stripped-back bare brickwork are central to the aesthetic of craft beer. Even more aspirational than that is the opportunity to drink in the brewery itself, somewhere on an industrial estate, sitting on utilitarian wooden benches beneath metal shelves piled high with bags and boxes, shiny stainless-steel vessels in the background and a forklift truck beeping in the distance.

Craft beer doesn't just *happen* to be centred in industrial locations; it celebrates the fact. It suggests something post- rather than pre-industrial, taking the detritus of the industrial age and re-appropriating it, repurposing it, reshaping old components into something new. There's a playfulness and anarchy among the spaces mainstream industry has abandoned, as if craft beer is playing among the ruins of a previous civilisation. Like all craft, craft beer is nostalgic. But it differs from other crafts in that it pines for the industrial age rather than the bucolic neverland industry supposedly killed off. Craft beer doesn't want to pre-date industry at all. Instead, it wants to pre-date the corporatisation that closed its grip on us in the 1970s. It wants to pre-date the age when the maximisation of shareholder value and the impossible promise of eternal growth sacrificed quality, integrity, and the dignity of the worker.

Chapter 7:
The computer says no

Have a nice day

A few weeks before the 2020 Covid-19 lockdown began, I was walking across the City of London with some time on my hands. I'd finished a meeting and had an event a mile or so away, so I decided to trace a weaving, meandering route, looking for a place to stop along the way.

This route took me past just one pub, almost at the end of my walk – and eight separate branches of the sandwich shop chain, Pret A Manger. In one of the busiest parts of London, I walked for over half an hour before I spotted a single pub. Most of the time, if I stood directly outside one branch of Pret, I could see the next one further along the road.

At first, I railed against this deadly combination of creeping neo-puritanism and insane corporate greed. City workers were once famous for their boozy lunches, but some financial firms have now declared a cheeky lunchtime pint to be a sackable offence. And Pret don't seem too far away now from turning that classic satirical headline from *The Onion* – "Starbucks opens new branch of Starbucks in Starbucks Restroom" – into a reality. The combination of no pubs and an obsessive number of Prets in the same space struck me as symptoms of a society suffering from mental illness.

And then I passed a row of windows at pavement level, which looked down onto an office floor that was about ten feet below. Inside, the windows would have been well above head height, affording limited daylight and an unending view of feet like mine, trudging past. The glass was covered with a film of black dots, providing a veil of partial privacy, and presumably halving the amount of natural light that was getting in. At 6pm on a dark and drizzly February night, the office was empty of people, but still lit by bleak halogen tubes, so I could see in clearly enough: grey carpet tiles, grey walls, grey chairs, grey everything. The whole place consisted of long lines of grey desks, in pairs of rows facing each other across low partitions, with a narrow space behind each row that was surely difficult to navigate once people were sitting in their chairs.

Each desk was about two-thirds of the width of the modest desk I'm sitting at as I write this at home, and about half the depth. Each was identical: a keyboard and an adjustable monitor whose flexible, black rubber-ribbed hinge made it look curiously alien and intrusive. I could see little or nothing else on most desks: certainly no personal effects, and nowhere to put them.

I was reminded of depictions of Dickensian offices full of clerks on TV and film. Maybe this office once looked like that. But those clerks had far more work space and more personal space than I was looking at here.

Then I thought of those eight Prets, and realised that few of them had any seating areas: they catered to people who worked like this, who queued for their sandwiches every lunchtime and brought them back to desks like these to eat them, presumably while answering emails.

Clearly, the people who design these workspaces couldn't give a shit about the happiness or comfort of the people who have to work in them. About half the British working population now works in open plan offices, compared to 23 per cent of workers globally.[99] While organisations trumpet

---

[99]https://workplaceinsight.net/open-plan-linked-fall-engagement-workplace-satisfaction/

the advantages for collaboration and efficiency, the true reason is cost: British office space is pricier than almost anywhere else. And as for those supposed productivity benefits, study after study confirms that not only are workers less happy in open plan offices, they are also less productive, less collaborative and less interactive than those in cubicles or separate offices. In a global survey of 12,000 office workers, British offices were found to be the ugliest and coldest in the world.[100]

When people were yoked together like this in factories as opposed to offices, there were trades unions campaigning to improve conditions for workers. Today's workers may be better paid, and the work may be less physically dangerous and strenuous, but the psychological conditions can't have improved much, and the satisfaction many people feel with their work is low.[101]

In the same way that machines and robots screwed manual workers in the 1970s, algorithms and the arrival of artificial intelligence (AI) are now shafting office workers. Offices like the one I walked past in the City are little better than the production lines we used to watch on *Play School*. The nature of work is undergoing profound change once again. Even before the coronavirus pandemic, many people who work in offices were being told that they were surplus to requirements. If it hasn't happened already, AI will soon be able to do what they do cheaper and more efficiently. As algorithms begin to replace journalists, we're entering the age of things being hand-written by robots.

Companies expect us to be loyal to the point of a religious calling. In many organisations, we're not just expected to turn up and offer a chunk of our time working in return for

---

[100]https://www.harpersbazaar.com/uk/people-parties/bazaar-at-work/news/a37368/british-offices-are-the-coldest-and-ugliest-in-the-world/
[101]https://royalsocietypublishing.org/doi/full/10.1098/rstb.2017.02 39

money: we're expected to live by the company's set of values. When I worked in a brand consultancy, we would do brand values workshops where we'd come up with words like "passionate", "committed" and "goes the extra mile", to describe the attitude or tone of voice of a company or brand, and sometimes these would find their way into appraisals and job reviews. It's not just enough to do your job well, you have to *think* correctly about it as well. In the end, this is why I couldn't do that job any more.

As far back as 1983, Arlie Hochschild coined the term "emotional labour" to describe this kind of management, where feelings, emotions and thoughts are bent to the company's commercial imperatives.[102] She studied flight attendants and debt collectors, noting that the former are expected to be "nicer than natural", and the latter "nastier than natural". She describes how a flight attendant can become estranged not only from how s/he expresses emotion – their smile is no longer "their" smile – but also from what s/he actually feels. Anyone who works in a service job who is disciplined or penalised for not smiling while dealing with sales calls, or not following a scripted exhortation to "have a nice day" or ask "is there anything else I can help you with today," is being estranged from their feelings just as the worker on a production line is estranged from the things they make.

Like the 1970s, the machines and the procedures, programmes and protocols surrounding them are not designed by the workers who have to use them. They represent decision-making and agency being taken away from workers and are therefore responsible for alienating them from their jobs and ultimately ripping the guts out of any sense of vocation or job satisfaction. We are expected to answer emails late at night and phone calls on holiday. Except we don't even call it "holiday" any more: so

---

[102]Hochschild, Arlie, *The Managed Heart: Commercialization of Human* Feeling (University of California, 2012.)

important is work in the 21st century, we've started calling our weeks off "leave" – a word that at once shifts the emphasis towards permission being granted rather than paid holiday as a statutory right, and makes it sound like we're all in the armed forces rather than working in telesales for Marks & Spencer's home and car insurance.

In return for our blind devotion and loyalty, we no longer get jobs for life or career paths, but unpaid internships, zero hours contracts and the gig economy. But that's OK, because we're not just "workers" any more, we're "colleagues," and that makes us equal, all in this together, all on the same team.

The crappy open-plan format of offices is merely the most visible aspect of a fashionable approach to working practices that is not only bad for the worker, but has more far-reaching effects. In *The Craftsman*, Richard Sennett relates studies which show that in a workshop or laboratory, speaking to people directly is far more effective than written instructions because it allows the message to be tailored and customised, and improved by feedback. So, naturally, in their ineffable wisdom, corporations rush to replace direct contact with email, text message, manuals, and on-line training modules. Sennett also cites multiple studies from around the world which prove that, when it comes to motivating workers in any environment to do a job well, there are two main approaches, equally unsuccessful. The idea of urging people to work collectively for the greater good, as is common in totalitarian states, creates massive demotivation and inefficiency. The idea of appealing to people as individuals who are competing with each other for promotions and pay rises – instilling the idea that in order for me to succeed, my co-worker must fail – demoralises and disillusions everyone apart from those who succeed in climbing to the top of the greasy pole. Sennett argues that the most effective way to get a job done – whether it's Linux computing, the invention of the mobile phone or the dynamics of an orchestra – is for people to collaborate in a spirit of openness and honesty, allowing workers agency and a collective responsibility for problem solving, not for some greater good, but for the success of the task at hand. Obviously then, our employers ignore this, dehumanising the workplace, instilling measurement and regulation wherever they can, siloing people in an atmosphere of uncertainty and mistrust where we have no power to question the way things are done, all summed up in the old *Little Britain* sketch where the "computer says no".

In this environment, we lose sight of what we are doing and why. The reliance on algorithms and computers is as deskilling in some senses as the machines of the industrial age were to manual labour. Sennett cites the example of the physicist Victor Weisskopf, who once said to his MIT students who worked exclusively with computerised experiments, "When you show me the result, the computer understands the answer, but I don't think you understand the answer".[103] This echoes *Shop Class as Soulcraft,* in which philosopher-turned-motorcycle-repairman Matthew Crawford quotes a Californian teacher of agriculture bemoaning the fact that "We have a generation of students that can answer questions on standardized tests, know factoids, but they can't do anything".[104]

When the "computer says no," we assume it must be right even if we have no idea why. This gives the illusion of certainty and allows the abdication of individual responsibility. We get to a point where, in the words of the stock defence at the Nuremberg trials, we're just following orders. The people our workplaces deal with stop being real people to us and become "shoppers," "consumers" or "members of the public" – just more numbers to be measured and analysed by the computer.

Behind all this, there's an underlying assumption that this

---

[103]Sennett, 2009, pp.39-45.
[104]Crawford, 2009, p.12.

new strain of scientific, quantitative management improves efficiency in the work place. The opposite is true, because fully-rounded human beings actually want to do something meaningful and have a desire to do it well. We don't just sell hours of our time to our employers: for those of us who want what we do to have some kind of meaning, work isn't working. When we meet people for the first time, "What do you do?" is the first question we ask. Our jobs are who we are, and increasingly, we don't like that person. In the UK in particular, where these practices are very firmly embedded, the idea that "we hardly do anything all day" at work is a national joke. Skiving is seen as a virtue. As a workforce we are disengaged, demoralised and cynical.

If that's how we feel about work, when we're away from the office we spend much of our lives gazing at screens of one kind of another, where the only manual labour many of us do is tapping or swiping, and we let algorithms make decisions for us on what to watch, listen to or read next. Something is missing from modern life in general – it's a problem with work, but not just work. As Peter Korn puts it, when talking about the people who sign up for his crafting courses, "The banquet of work, leisure and consumption that society prescribes has left some essential part of them undernourished. They are hungry for the avenues of engagement that provide more wholesome sustenance".[105]

The reunification of hand and head

Korn's choice of diet and sustenance as a metaphor is an interesting one. The void that many of us feel inside is curious and difficult to describe. In this way, the whole modern experience mirrors the highly processed Western diet; overloaded with salt and fat and lacking in actual nutrients. As Michael Pollan showed in his analysis of modern food supply, *In Defence of Food*, it's the only diet in

---

[105]Korn, 2017, p.10

the world that will make you ill if you stick to it exclusively.[106]

Peter Korn starts his book *Why We Make Things and Why It Matters* with the question, "Why do we choose the spiritually, emotionally and physically demanding work of bringing new objects into the world with creativity and skill?"[107] Asked in those terms, the answer seems almost rhetorical. But if Korn left it to speak for itself we wouldn't have his wonderful book, towards the end of which he reflects that the craft of furniture-making may not be a "cure-all" for the sense of alienation and demotivation we feel in our lives, but that it "functions as a source of meaning, authenticity, fulfilment – call it what you will for the moment... what lures [my students] is the hope of finding a deeper meaning by learning to make things well with their own hands".[108]

For Peter Korn's chairs, you could substitute any number of activities done by hand. I've always been physically clumsy, struggling with everything from sport to DIY to the mystical art of coopering. When you decide you aren't physically adept, it becomes a self-fulfilling condition. While I was researching *The Apple Orchard,* I challenged this. I went on a course to learn how to graft apple trees, which is a perfect example of a craft skill in the way it requires head and hand to work together. My first attempt at grafting, where you cut partially through the stem of one plant and splice a cutting from a different plant into it, was unexpectedly successful. But when I started overthinking what I was doing, I became worse at doing it, so I tried to approach it in a different way. Instead of looking down at my hands from above, I tried to move my consciousness, my sense of self, down *into* my hands themselves. Immediately I become steadier, more patient. My breathing

---

[106]Pollan Michael, *In Defence of Food* (Penguin, London, 2009)
[107]Korn, 2017, p.7.
[108]Ibid. p.10.

slowed and I relaxed. My pruning knife, which I had been handling clumsily, became an extension of me rather than my enemy. I started making the right kinds of cuts, and no longer felt clumsy. It was the first time I could remember feeling physically confident.

After about six years of baking sourdough bread, I've arrived at a similar place. My intellectual curiosity in the behaviour of wild yeasts means I understand why I'm doing all the steps I have to do. But it's the feeling in my fingertips, the sensation of a certain silkiness and pliability in the dough, that tells me when it's had enough kneading and stretching and is ready to rise. There's a point at which I know whether it's going to turn out well or not which I could never explain in words. The Turkish baker just around the corner from my house sells excellent sourdough loaves for £2.99 – not that much more than the cost of the flour I buy to make my own. Their loaves are far better than most of my attempts, and it would take me less than five minutes to go to the shop and return with one. But that's not the point of my baking: the reason I make sourdough is to reconnect with physical sensations, to unify hand and head in a way I've rarely experienced before, bringing an end to the false Cartesian separation of body and mind. Okay, I'll admit: I am a North London middle-class, middle-aged man, so I also make sourdough specifically so that so I can post pictures of my freshly baked loaves on Instagram. But destroying the false Cartesian separation of body and mind is the main reason I do it. Far more important. Honest.

Doing things with our hands has become aspirational, because it's something we don't get to do very often without making a specific effort. For people who don't like sourdough, the answer might be spoon carving. For French documentary maker Benjamin Carle, it was making a sandwich. In 2017, Carle decided to really *make* a sandwich, from scratch. He dug a plot of land to grow the wheat to bake the bread, pressed olives for their oil, and went out on

159

a Basque fishing boat to catch some tuna. "My girlfriend knits and I saw all around me more and more people who have nice day jobs but spend their evenings doing some kind of manual activity and telling the rest of us about it," he told *The Guardian*. "We are all in DIY-mode. It's as if our intellectual jobs are too abstract and not satisfying enough. People are happier with some kind of material reality". The whole process took him ten months, and he filmed it for a documentary which he called *Sandwich (or How I Made My Own Snack While Questioning the Manual Capabilities of the French and While Trying to Find Some Personal Pride)*.[109]

The need to do something with our hands, and the sense of fulfilment we get from doing so, has grown in direct proportion to the amount of time we spend looking at screens and losing ourselves in virtual worlds. It's easy to explain in terms of how our work and leisure time are evolving. But there's a scientific reason behind our urge to get physical.

The human brain has now been mapped, and neuroscientists have been able to show what parts of the brain are responsible for which functions. One interesting product of the mapping of the cerebral cortex is that we now know how much of the brain we devote to sensory information from various parts of our bodies. Wilder Penfield, an American brain surgeon, performed experiments on the brains of epileptics while they were in surgery, and successfully calibrated not just the areas of the brain where different functions are performed, but how much of that area was involved. In 1954, he devised the "cortical homunculus", a re-imagining of the human body as it would look if each body part corresponded in size to the amount of the brain devoted to it.

---

[109] https://www.theguardian.com/world/2018/mar/04/benjamin-carle-frenchman-sandwich-quest-fulfilment

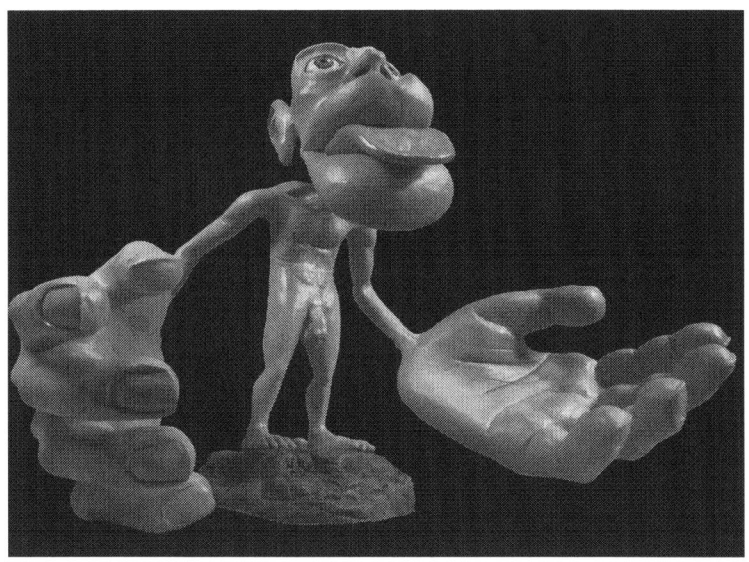

More of our brains are devoted to sensory stimulus from the hands than any other part of the body. If we're not touching anything more than a keyboard or a screen, it's a form of sensory deprivation.

And so, we watch *Bake Off, Pottery Throwdown, Sewing Bee, Repair Shop* and *Back in Time* for inspiration. When we turn the TV off, we're getting into pottery, weaving, even that 1970s classic, macramé, all fuelled in no small part by millennials showing off their creations on Instagram. The retailer Hobbycraft has posted nine straight years of sales growth and is opening new stores across the UK, with a total of 94 shops and an increase in online sales of 22.7% in 2019.[110]

Modern interest in craft then, is a response to two separate but closely linked phenomena: the need to work with our hands and engage with the world physically; and the desire for freedom from an over-regulated, algorithm-dominated work and leisure space. So we might ask a question as

---

[110]https://www.retailgazette.co.uk/blog/2019/07/hobbycraft-revenue-surpasses-100m-thanks-online-sales/

rhetorical as the one Peter Korn asked earlier: why on earth would someone with a sophisticated knowledge of spreadsheets who sits at a computer all day in a cramped open-plan office with people they don't like want to throw it all away, swap their suit for a pair of overalls and switch to mashing in and making beer?

This is anecdotal rather than statistical, but whenever I ask a craft brewer what they were doing before they started their brewery, they're far more likely to say IT or finance than any other career. It's easy to see why. Academic (and real ale fan) Tom Thurnell-Read has been exploring this phenomenon from a socio-cultural point of view for several years. In 2014, Tom published a paper called *Craft, tangibility and affect at work in the microbrewery*. He interviewed around twenty brewers. One spoke of the mental stress of his previous job in education, and how it used to drain him of energy:

> I was, as most of my colleagues were, under a lot of stress and not everybody admitted that and I think I just went through years and years of stress without realising it and it catches up with you in the end and that used to tire me out, the mental stress of the job. Now, it's the physical side of this job that tires me out and it is taking a toll on my body because it's all lifting 25 kilo sacks of grain, it is full nine-gallon casks of beer. So, I mean, that's taken a bit of a toll, but I don't have any stress any more.[111]

Becoming a craft brewer allows you to make something meaningful during your work time. There's a great scene in Tom Wolfe's 1987 novel *Bonfire of the Vanities* where Sherman McCoy, bond trader and self-proclaimed "Master of the Universe," takes his family to the beach. Sherman's eight-year-old daughter Campbell is playing with some friends when she rushes back to him with an urgent question: *what does daddy do?* MacKenzie's daddy makes

---

[111]Thurnell-Read, Tom, "Craft, tangibility and affect at work in the microbrewery," published in *Emotion, Space and Society*, (Vol.13, 2014.)

books. What does Sherman make? In trying to explain bonds, he talks about raising money that might be used for building schools and hospitals. Campbell leaps on this and asks which roads and hospitals daddy has built. Well, no specific ones... then his wife tries an analogy – think of a bond as a cake – daddy collects crumbs from all the cakes he handles and they add up to a big pile. Daddy makes cakes? Well, no... Campbell is soon in tears, inconsolable, and no one is really any the wiser as to what Sherman actually does at work all day.

It's a scene that's echoed any time someone asks the ambiguous question, "What do you make?" For many craft brewers, the physical interpretation of this question became more important than the financial one. In making that choice, these people were directly challenging the prevailing orthodoxy of western capitalism: that financial success is the most meaningful measure of value. Choosing to follow a different path can be as much a political statement as a personal one. As Peter Korn points out, "Prior to the Industrial Revolution, virtually every object had been produced 'by hand'. Subsequent to it, making things by hand became a potentially subversive act – something one did in opposition to prevailing societal norms".[112]

The value and values of craft brewing

Making something by hand, and choosing to prioritise an alternative source of value above financial success, are the acts of the modern-day Outsider, and together they explain the allure of craft beer for both the makers and drinkers of it. Tom Thurnell-Read found that both themes ran consistently through the attitudes of the brewers he interviewed:

> In terms of being a successful brewer, two themes were predominant. Firstly, brewers spoke of the process of acquiring

---

[112]Korn, 2017, p.96.

and putting into practice knowledge and skills. Thus, a detailed understanding of the brewing process coupled with the proper use of materials, ingredients and equipment were seen as prerequisites of success in the trade. Secondly, a more subjective, affective and impressionistic sense of passion for the craft was evident in all interviewees' accounts.[113]

We might characterise this by saying we expect a brewer to brew good craft beer, and also to behave like a good craft brewer. Thurnell-Read's research confirmed a narrative that I've witnessed consistently over the last decade: if only one of these is present – either one – the person is not a "real" craft brewer. I'd go as far as to say that many craft beer brewers and drinkers find it easier to excuse the production of poor-quality craft beer than they do the failure to behave within the norms that have been established by the craft beer scene.

In 2017, Atlanta brewery Scofflaw made a statement on its Facebook page attacking fans who had complained about the variability in its beers, with one customer noting that different cans in the same six-pack of IPA tasted like entirely different beers. The post in response featured a photograph of the entire brewery team raising their middle fingers at the reader, blamed inconsistency on their equipment, size and their inability to source the best ingredients, and closed with the sentence, "Don't think this is professional, well that's good cause I am not a professional, I am a fucking scofflaw."

Fans waded in on both sides of the debate. Where they were critical of Scofflaw's stance, they were also mostly conciliatory beginning with: "I take your point…" or "I'm a big fan of your beers, but…" Scofflaw's responses were hostile, with one ending "we will not be bullied."[114]

---

[113]Thurnell-Read 2014
[114]https://www.pastemagazine.com/drink/scofflaw-brewing/breweries-vs-fans-craft-beer-on-social-media/

Craft beer fans largely accept inconsistency as part of the deal. The outcry that followed Scofflaw's outburst went around the craft beer world, and ultimately focussed more, if anything, on the arrogance and confrontational attitude that didn't fit craft beer's behavioural norms rather than the fact that the brewery was making poor-quality beer. A few days later the brewery issued a clarification that was almost, but not quite, an apology, insisting that the picture of the team collectively giving the finger to their fans was not, in fact, a picture of the team collectively giving the finger to their fans at all. They reassured us that they were committed to making the best beer possible, but crucially, that they were also committed to "craft values".[115]

Craft beer is a counter-cultural movement. It has its own language, with hopheads drinking awesome, crushable beers, whether they be juice bombs, hazy bois or whales, all while trying their best to avoid shelf turds and drain pours. It has its own visual aesthetic, which borrows heavily from heavy metal and indie rock – both counter-cultural themselves – to such an extent that extravagant beards and sleeve tats are used by craft cynics as an attempt to write the whole thing off as a hipster fad. Craft beer fashion may be a cliché, but so is wearing a suit and tie to the office, and craft is self-consciously distancing itself from that as much as it can.

Craft has developed its own beer styles, and its own visual identity in both products and packaging – the popularity of hazy, juicy beers may have been driven by Instagram, but beer's problem was always that, once your pint of premium lager was poured into a generic glass, no one could see what a discerning choice of brand you'd made. While the mainstream has invested heavily in branded glassware, craft has made sure that anyone can see you're drinking craft beer just by looking at its contents.

---

[115]https://www.craftbeer.com/featured-brewery/atlanta-scofflaw-brewing-facebook-photo

But more important than all these image-based characteristics, craft beer behaves differently from the mainstream. Craft is more progressive in its politics – craft beer bars are more likely to have gender-neutral toilets than mainstream pubs, craft beer design and advertising is less far likely to fall back on tired sexist tropes, and craft drinkers and brewers are more likely to talk about issues from mental health to racism. That's not to say the industry is free from racism, bullying or abuse – or a much commented-upon "bro culture" – but when it occurs, it gets called out publicly and volubly.

In business practice, craft beer is built on openness and collaboration, just like Richard Sennett suggests. Behaving like a good craft brewer means not just being passionate about brewing craft beer, but also being respectful of your customers, drinkers and peers, demonstrating ethical and progressive values, loaning kit or ingredients, sharing advice, even creating co-branded collaborative brews. This stands in stark contrast to the mainstream, where several different brewers for one giant corporate (guess who?) in different parts of the world, who do not know one another, have each individually told me that it is "a career-ending move" to be seen drinking a competitor's beer in public, even if you're off the clock, on holiday or on your friend's stag night.

This is why people on the craft beer scene really get upset when a craft brewer such as Beavertown or Goose Island sells in part or whole to a major corporate. Going back to our duality of purpose, critics of such moves often rationalise their disapproval that x corporation will stop making good craft beer – that they will start insisting on using cheaper ingredients, make the beer blander to suit broader mainstream tastes, or otherwise compromise. But the true source of ire is that the brewer in question is no longer behaving like a good craft brewer.

As well as selling out altogether, a craft brewer might start

166

selling beer through supermarkets, where it will be sold at prices craft beer's own routes to market can't compete with. They might run an advertising campaign that is seen as too "slick". Or they might just grow too big. Each of these is interpreted a sign that the craft brewer is backsliding into mainstream cultural norms, prioritising profit over craft principles.

Handmade by automation

Since 2006, I've been part of a perpetual, global conversation about craft beer that established itself with its own rules. It began with blogs, which thrived in part because mainstream media refused to engage with people who wanted to write about beer, further cementing the feeling that we were counter-cultural. This exploded with the arrival of Twitter and Facebook, and continues today via online magazines, Instagram, UnTappd, podcasts and more, breaking off into endless subgroups and communities. A great deal of the everyday chatter in this conversation is about excitedly sharing news of the latest rare beer release, but when conversation turns to exploring the nature of craft beer more broadly, it invariably focuses far more on the cultural aspects of being a good craft beer brewer or drinker than it does on the embodied nature of craft beer, the way it is made.

Craft beer has prospered in a digital environment, and while the physical nature of craft and the innate appeal of "hand-crafted" products still appeal at least in an abstract sense, the physical reality of how the beer was made seems to have become a secondary consideration, less important than the cultural norms of behaving like a good craft brewer. I've only ever found Charlie Papazian's definition of a craft brewery as "any brewery using the manual arts and skills of a brewer to create its products," in articles discussing the history of the term "craft beer", rather than any contemporary discussion of what a craft brewery is today.

167

So if craft is "a self-conscious counter-point to factory-made goods", can genuine craft products ever be made in factory conditions?

Earlier, we explored this question with respect to the sparging arm on top of a mash tun – one of the simplest pieces of technology in the brewing world. In October 2019, I got to the chance to explore a far more complex example of the issue.

I spent Halloween 2019 at BrewDog's ambitious brewery/bar/hotel complex on the outskirts of Columbus, Ohio. After spending a night in "The Doghouse", I was given a tour of the main plant. The brewery is state-of-the-art. After a spacious laboratory, we were shown a wall of gleaming silver pipes. Everything is enclosed at every step of the brewing process. Next, we visited the control room. A bank of computer screens showed the whole brewery in diagram form. From here, ingredients can be added, boilers turned on, valves opened and closed, all at the touch of a button. The labour of making beer is as removed from human intervention as it possibly can be. The brewers make no bones about it: "Our entire brewery is automated," they told us proudly. "Everything stays in the pipes – there are over three miles of pipes in the brewery."

The brewers here don't get to see the beer they are brewing until they open a can of the finished product. Once the process is underway, there's very little they can do to intervene or put their own mark on it. The principle here, of brewers directing the entire process from a room full of computer terminals, is exactly the same as I've seen at the main Stella Artois brewery in Leuven, Belgium, albeit on a slightly smaller scale.

So can BrewDog Ohio in any way be called a craft brewery?

There are plenty who would give a resounding "no". BrewDog are like the small indie band you saw playing in a club who are now touring stadia. The sense of finding something special, something secret, has evaporated.

But BrewDog is scrupulous about conforming to the American definition of a craft brewer. More relevantly, everyone we met at the brewery conformed to every single aspect of the counter-cultural norms of being a good craft brewer. They were humble, kind, friendly, and displayed none of the arrogance that some craft beer geeks feel the BrewDog brand now embodies. Also, the brewery is still turning out beers that, on their own merits, are of consistently good quality and of a character that fits exactly with our expectations of what a craft beer should look and taste like.

It's always easy to pick on BrewDog, just as it is in any market or sphere of life where someone local has become far bigger and more successful than most of their peers. Their every move is scrutinised and criticized no matter what it is. But pretty much any craft brewery exists at a point on a scale between being fully automated and entirely hand-crafted. Many thriving breweries have a large, automated brewhouse and a small pilot kit. Are they craft or not? Are beers made using the pilot kit craft, and beers from the main brewhouse not? What if they brew the same beer on both kits and they turn out identical? From the outside, how do you tell which is craft and which is not?

We're getting back to the point where attempts at tight definitions lead to the absurd. And this happens in broader discussions of craft – not just in beer. If an artist, a designer or a sculptor uses digital technology to create their work instead of their hands, can they truly be called an artist or craftsperson?

Obviously there are different takes on this, not least within communities of craftspeople. But there is a compelling argument for the "digital artisan" movement. In the introduction to *Digitally Handmade* (2015) – a book that

169

showcases work created by artists and craftspeople using a mixture of traditional crafts and new technologies that cluster loosely under the term "3D-printing" – author Lucy Johnson argues that the contrasting approaches of artistic creativity and "the ever-rational nature of computer technologies" can, in the right hands, liberate a creative person rather than entrapping them. Mastering these tools can lead to a level of ideas and execution that were not possible before. The first person featured in the book, textile artist Jekaterina Apale, says that working with a digital loom is "almost not like weaving at all – it is more like painting with threads. There is so much potential to be creative with the process itself, not just the initial pattern design".[116]

In a sense, it was always thus – craftspeople have always used the best tools they can get hold of to do the job at hand. Back in the mid-eighteenth century, when pondering this question, Denis Diderot argued that "The enlightened way to use a machine is to judge its powers, fashion its uses, in light of our own limits rather than the machine's potential".[117] The great critique of the Industrial Revolution and the subdivision of scientifically managed labour that followed was never the existence of the machines themselves; it was the way those machines were used to separate people from any meaningful sense of control over their labour, or engagement with the products of it. If makers are in complete control of the tools, machines and technology at their disposal, free to make whatever they like with it, then we either allow this to be called craft, or we condemn craft to drift increasingly into the past.

I began this book by following attempts to define "craft beer". These originated as multi-facted ideals that didn't survive contact with the real world, and ended up in a place

---

[116]Johnston, Lucy, *Digitally Handmade* (Thames & Hudson, London, 2015) p.11 reference
[117]Diderot summed up by Sennett, 2017, p.105.

where "independence" was the only meaningful metric. The attachment to the word "craft" had begun to loosen. I then laid out an argument that independence of ownership – while being an important issue in its own right – really isn't the most important thing to think about when trying to decide whether or not a beer or brewery is "craft".

By placing craft beer firmly within a conversation about the broader craft movement, it turns out that independence is a very important factor in craft after all, but not in the way the brewing industry talks about it. More important than what kind of entity owns the brewery is whether the brewer has independence of action – are they free to brew the beers they want in the way they see fit using whatever level of technology they feel like using? Are they working in an environment that's the opposite of "computer says no", where the technology works for them rather than the other way around?

The brewers at BrewDog Ohio spoke passionately about the beers they had designed, and the pride they felt at brewing them on such state-of-the-art kit. And then we went next door to the sour beer facility, where beers ferment in wooden barrels using techniques and ingredients that have changed little over the past few centuries.

Some craft breweries inevitably take on some characteristics of mainstream breweries. Also, some big, commercial breweries are now adopting characteristics we'd associate more readily with craft breweries. Craft and mainstream are in constant flow. Taking Colin Wilson's concept of the Outsider and the Bourgeois, particularly the way in which they are mutually dependent, we can use it to show how craft producers and mainstream producers similarly enjoy co-dependency. Taking this idea further, they don't just need each other; they interact and change each other. Craft exists as a necessary reaction against, and vital alternative to, mainstream corporatisation and homogenisation. But these two positions have a dialectical relationship, the moves of

171

each affecting the next turn of the other. It's hardly surprising that some craft brewers grow, and some big brewers take an interest in craft. It's impossible for them to remain separate.

After pulling apart the definition of craft beer, we've spent the core of this book talking about craft generally rather than beer specifically, and now we're looping back, closing the circle. We've looked at a lot of subjects – practical and theoretical, manual and mental – that may initially seem like they don't have much to do with craft beer directly. We've only touched on the history of beer while exploring the history of craft in some detail. But when we get to the present, we can see that the current fascination with craft beer comes not from an interest in the machinations of the brewing industry, but from the nature and attraction of craft as an idea.

Craft brewing associations around the world may be retreating from the word "craft" itself, and I applaud any efforts to protect an independent brewing industry from the insatiable hunger of corporations. But the idea of craft is so much broader and richer than that. It taps into not just the innate appeal of supporting small, local, more idealistic businesses and drinking beers that have character, but the way we interact with the world around us, the way we see ourselves, and how we choose to live our lives in a much wider sense. This is why we need to retain the word "craft", to rescue it as a meaningful term, and to continue to use it to describe this incredible movement in the beer world.

Part Three:
"Craft Beer" is absolutely essential

Chapter 8:
"All the best words"

This might sound weird, but when I first started writing, I didn't think I was all that interested in words.

I had ideas and stories I wanted to communicate, and knew that I was better at doing that in writing than I was in any other medium. But I started off by just hammering the words down. It didn't matter if they were the best words, or if the sound they made in my head as they ran after each other was the most pleasing they could make. So long as it was clear and coherent, I thought, it would do.

But you can't work closely with any medium without evolving an intimate knowledge of it. Just as a furniture maker develops an ever-deeper relationship with wood, getting to know the flow of its grain and the density of its fibres, and how it's likely to behave under certain conditions, so I became increasingly fascinated by the texture and rhythm of different words, obsessing over why one word fits better in a sentence than another, or why the word "biscuit" in the punchline of one of my favourite jokes makes it way funnier than the words "cake" or "chocolate" would.

This love of words has been fed by my growing appreciation and knowledge of beer. At the risk of contradicting Donald Trump, brewing has all the best words: "sparging", "mash tun," "trub", "brewhouse," "Maris Otter", "Fuggles" and, more than any other term, "grist case": each stands out like a cheeky thumbs-up from a good friend in any sentence they occupy.

I think this is why I'm more obsessed with the endless

debate around craft beer than is probably healthy. I like the words "craft beer" a great deal, both individually and together. Every time I hear them, they create a smile in my mind. If I knew a bit more about neuroscience than the smattering I've learned for my beer and music matching show, I'd probably be able to describe how the sound of them fires synapses in my mind or releases endorphins, like Pavlov's bell. It's not just the anticipation of the imminent pleasure of piney hops against a solid malty backbone; it's a set of ideas, feelings and associations that have become deeply linked to the sight or sound of those two words together.

I think I first used the term "craft beer" in my second book, *Three Sheets to the Wind* (2006), following my first visit to the Oregon Beer Festival in 2004. It didn't have an "official" definition by that point, and yet I knew exactly what it meant. My idea of what it means has changed since then, but language is fluid and alive, and words change their meanings over time. "Nice" used to mean "foolish" or "simple", while "silly" once meant "worthy" or "blessed". "Guy" entered language as a general noun rather than a person's name after people made effigies of Guy Fawkes and named them after him. It evolved to mean any kind of frightful figure, then a man, and during my lifetime, it has grown to encompass people of any gender. "Fizzle" began life as a term for a quiet fart.

I've never believed that words need to have tight, singular, universally agreed definitions in order to be carriers of meaning between people. I was delighted to discover that the word "definition" itself has various different definitions, which kind of says it all.

People seek definitions for different reasons. We don't actually need to know the definition of something to understand what it is. I often illustrate this by asking people to define what a giraffe is. They immediately start talking about a four-legged animal with a long neck, but that's a *description* of a giraffe rather than a *definition* of one. To the extent that it has been described so far, it also works a definition of a donkey or a llama. The definition of a giraffe is that it is a species of even-toed ungulate (Artiodactyla), which are themselves a class of mammal, while donkeys belong to the Equus family of Perissodactyla, a different order of the class mammalia. In definitional terms, the key difference between a giraffe and a donkey is that giraffes spread their weight evenly across all their toes, while donkeys don't. I didn't know that until I looked it up. But I've always been able to tell the difference between a giraffe and a donkey, and I don't think this new (to me) information about their toes is going to make any difference at all to how I think about them.

It is perhaps unfair to compare two very different-looking mammals to the craft beer debate, because while most of us can easily tell a giraffe and a donkey apart, the reason many people yearn for a clear, workable definition of craft beer is so that they can shine light into the grey areas where something they believe is not a craft beer is trying to pass itself off as one, and the difference is not as obvious. Many have belatedly realised that attempts to use a term as rich in meaning and association as craft beer will always fail, because trying to define it for this purpose is a reductive and self-defeating exercise. The word "independent" works far better on this score.

My argument, then, is that the term "craft beer" is not fit for the purpose the craft brewing industry has been trying to use it. My belief is that while it may have failed in that job, it is still useful in a much bigger way, to describe and evoke a powerful movement in the brewing and consumption of beer, and to locate beer rightfully within a broader tradition of craft, a set of ideas and approaches which help us live more meaningfully in the world.

I'd like to propose that when we do talk about craft beer, instead of focusing on size and ownership as ways of

177

defining it, we instead look at other attributes of craft that hold it to account, keep it honest and give it meaning. These are the things we should really be focusing on if we want craft beer – not just the term, but also the culture and products it describes – to survive and prosper in the decades to come. This may not be an exhaustive list, but the main attributes that I'd suggest rebuilding our ideas of craft beer around are:

1. Skill and creativity
2. Quality
3. Autonomy
4. Motivation

1. Skill and creativity

As we explored in part two, the notion of skill is at the very centre of what it means to be any kind of craft maker. We looked at how skills are acquired, and how innate knowledge, which goes so deep we can mistake it for instinct, is in fact the result of thousands of hours of practice. The idea of a long, dedicated apprenticeship has always been a defining feature of anything we now think of as a craft vocation.

Skill is so strongly connected to our ideas of craft beer that we just assume it's there. We are wrong to do so.

As a drinker and beer communicator, if I want to call myself a beer sommelier or cicerone, I have to spend quite a lot of money and many hours of my time studying and sitting exams in order to get the qualification. If I want to call myself a craft brewer, I just need to buy a brewing kit and make a beer on it. George Sturt quickly discovered that craft skills couldn't be picked up quickly just because you were well-educated – craft skill begins with apprenticeship. Richard Sennett writes that medieval guilds were structured in three tiers. As a boy you were apprenticed to a master for seven years, in a relationship that was so close it even took on attributes of parenting. After graduating as an apprentice, you worked as a journeyman craftsman, plying your trade wherever you could, still learning. This lasted for around ten years before a journeyman could finally attempt to prove himself the equal of a master.

There are formal apprenticeship schemes in brewing, but there's no obligation for anyone to sign up to them. I propose that there should be. I know many craft brewers who devise their own journey from apprentice to journeyman, starting by hanging around breweries or doing the cleaning and gradually picking up knowledge along the way. Others will brew tirelessly and obsessively on home brew kit before trading up. But there are plenty of "craft brewers" who are too impatient or lazy to do so, and we have no way of knowing that they've skipped the development of brewing skill until you take a mouthful of a faulty beer that has been intentionally over-hopped to hide its flaws. The craft brewing industry is investing heavily in marques or seals that certify a beer as the product of an independent brewery. I've seen no suggestion of a similar marque assuring drinkers that the beer has been brewed by someone who knows what they're doing because they've put the hours in to learn brewing skills to a higher than average level. If craft beer is to continue to thrive, this needs to be remedied.

With access to more resources, it's actually more likely that qualified, skilful brewers will be found in big breweries rather than small operations: Anheuser-Busch has a reputation for hiring the best students straight out of graduation from the brewing school at UC Davis in California. And this is why I've put skill together with creativity.

I was once asked by a major international brewer to give a talk and tutored tasting to their marketing department, focusing on beer styles. I replied that I was more than happy to take their money to do so, but expressed some surprise that they weren't asking their brewers to do the talk instead.

They replied that their brewers had only ever brewed one beer in their professional lives – the mainstream lager the company was famous for. They were outstandingly skilful in brewing that one beer, but knew no more than the marketers did about other beer styles.

Brewing a major international lager, then, is the perfect example of how division of labour can work at an institutional level to deskill a brewer in some areas while building skills to a world-class degree in a narrow field. By contrast, any competent craft brewer will be constantly exploring different beer styles and building up a much broader-based knowledge of the principles of brewing. This in turn feeds their creativity. When a brewer can see how ingredients combine in different ways in different styles, they start creating hybrids of those styles, and then new styles of beer altogether.

This interplay of skill and creativity is what many of us have come to expect from a good craft brewer, and among the craft brewers I know, the point at which they are combining skill and creativity is when I see them at their happiest. A brewer who creates nothing but an endless succession of hazy, juicy IPAs, not because they want to drink these beers themselves but because "that's what's really selling right now," is no more of a craft brewer than the person stuck at the big brand lager brewery.

2. Quality

During his own meditations on craft, Peter Korn quotes Robert M Persig, author of *Zen and the Art of Motorcyle Maintenance* (1974), who believed that a good life may be found through craftsman-like engagement with the actions, objects, and relationships of ordinary experience, by caring about what you do and making it nicer than it has to be. It's interesting that he uses the phrase "ordinary experience", and I wonder if this plays into the extent of the appeal of craft beer in particular. There hasn't been a "craft wine" boom because wine doesn't need one: most people who drink it already believe a high degree of skill and passion have gone into the making of it. Craft beer allows us to reconnect with something very ordinary in a much more meaningful way – that gives it its authenticity. It comes with an implicit understanding that craft beer – like any other crafted product – will be of uncommonly high quality when compared with the standardised, homogenised products of the industrial mainstream.

As we've seen, this is sometimes true and sometimes not. The technological revolution that hit brewing in the 1870s and 1880s was all about improving the quality of beer, and it was led by the largest brewers of the day. At some point, as overall demand for beer fell and big brewing became a battle for market share, the application of technology began to have more to do with making beer faster and cheaper rather than improving its quality.

A perfect example of this is Stella Artois. When I worked on its advertising campaign in the late 1990s, Stella was still a decent pilsner-style lager. It scored top in branded taste tests against other leading big brands because we'd managed to make the brand very desirable, but it scored bottom in blind taste tests against the same beers, because it had more bitterness and a more assertive flavour than the interchangeable beers it was up against. During the "Reassuringly Expensive" campaign of the 1980s, the agency ran a press ad with the headline "My shout, he whispered." The copy underneath explained why Stella was more expensive than other lagers. Apart from the higher ABV, which incurred more duty, the ad explained that it was made with traditional floor-malted barley, hopped exclusively with whole flower Saaz hops, contained no other cheaper adjuncts, and therefore conformed to the *Reinheitsgebot*, and was lagered for at least thirty days. Today, that sounds like a perfect description of a craft lager to me.

Not a single one of these points is true of Stella Artois any more, and the ABV of the beer has been lowered twice in recent years. Stella is a textbook example of how a product can be asset-stripped as the size and ambition of the company that owns it inflate to a global scale. I've already laid out why this doesn't always happen to a beer owned by a multinational corporation, but it's not an unreasonable assumption to make that the quality and integrity of a beer might not be near the top of a big brewer's list of priorities.

Just as we assume this about big brewers, we also assume that beers from craft brewers will be of high quality. Because they care, right?

Well, not always. More than once, when I've bought a craft beer that wasn't great, and then spoken to the brewer about it, they've said, "Yeah, we're still working on it, we're not quite happy with it," or "I know, we did have some issues with that batch," and I want to yell, "Why have I just paid six quid for it then?"

The idea of high quality never crops up in any attempted definition of craft beer. It's assumed. But it needs to be more explicit – it needs to be a promise craft beer makes rather than an unspoken expectation from the drinker. Otherwise, it doesn't conform to our general understanding of craft in its broad sense.

But in order to do that in a useful way, we also need to bottom out the relationship between quality and consistency.

Big Beer's defence of blandness is that for brands of such colossal size, consistency is paramount. This is perfectly valid. Consistency is the bedrock on which large brands are built. If you buy Heinz Tomato Ketchup, a Big Mac or a can of Coca-Cola, you expect every single one to taste the same as the last. If there's variability, brands such as these cannot make meaningful promises to the audiences of millions who consume them. When I was working on the malt section for *Miracle Brew*, I was initially surprised to learn that the specification for malt bought by Molson Coors to brew Carling was far stricter and more exacting than that for malt bought by any British craft brewer. "If you're brewing craft beer you can get away with a bit of haze, and variations in flavour are often celebrated," Jerry Dyson, Molson Coors's chief UK malt buyer told me. "But for a brand like Carling, that would be catastrophic. So, craft brewers sometimes buy the barley we reject."

In any advanced western economy, most of us who buy crafted products in some areas buy mainstream products in others. I'd feel uncomfortable buying, say, craft AA batteries or craft paracetamol. I'm not looking for any variation or inconsistency there. But as Jerry says, variation and fluctuation in craft production is celebrated, and always has been. Why? As usual, Richard Sennett sums it up perfectly:

> ...against the rigorous perfection of the machine, the craftsman became an emblem of human individuality, this emblem composed concretely by the positive value placed on variations, flaws, and irregularities in handwork... the sheer quantity of uniform objects aroused concerns that number would dull the senses, the uniform perfection of machined goods issuing no sympathetic invitation, no personal response.[118]

John Ruskin wanted his students to savour the irregularities of hand-made artefacts such as stained glass, and Diderot's *Enyclopedia* argued that in glassblowing, the imperfections and flaws, the tiny bubbles that differed from one glass to another, gave each glass a unique character.

The comparison with blown glass is particularly helpful in marking out the difference between quality and consistency. A set of four commercially available hand-blown wine glasses will typically start somewhere between £20 and £30 in the UK, while their industrially produced equivalents, of a

---

[118]Sennett, 2017, p84.

similar size and shape, can be bought for as little as £6 for four. We place a commercial value on the tiny variations from one glass to the next, because they are evidence that the glasses are hand-made. But crucially, each individual glass works just as well in its functional capacity as a wine glass as the next one does. They look like part of a set – if not identical, then obviously members of the same family. While they may vary in character, they are all of equal quality. If one of them leaked, or another wouldn't stand up because the base wasn't straight, we wouldn't say, "Ah well, it's craft, we should expect some inconsistencies." We'd take them back to the store or the manufacturer. And if they said, "Yeah, we're still working on it, we're not quite happy with it," or "I know, we did have some issues with that batch," we'd probably suggest they used their glasses in more creative and possibly painful ways than trying to flog them at a premium price point.

We want crafted products to bear the imprint of the individual who made them. But we also expect that individual to be good at making them. On the final page of *Cooked* (2013) – my favourite book about food – Michael Pollan learns how to make kimchi, and the Korean friend teaching him talks about the difference between "tongue taste" and "hand taste". Tongue taste is the straightforward chemical experience that takes place whenever anything makes contact with your taste buds. Hand taste is quite different:

> Hand taste involves something greater than mere flavour. It is the infinitely more complex experience of a food that bears the unmistakable signature of the individual who made it – the care and thought and idiosyncrasy that that person has put into the work of preparing it. Hand taste cannot be faked, Hyon Hee insisted, and hand taste is the reason we go to all this trouble, massaging the individual leaves of each cabbage and then folding them and packing them in the urn just so. What hand taste is, I understood all at once, is the taste of love.[119]

---

[119]Pollan, Michael, *Cooked: A Natural History of Transformation*

Going back to find this passage, I see that when I first read it five years ago, I scribbled in the margin, "And in the final paragraph, he defines craft beer!"

It feels an awfully long way from "I am not a professional, I am a fucking scofflaw."

3. Autonomy

When a craft brewer is swallowed up by a large corporation, there are two separate issues. The first is that some people want to support small, independent breweries as a cause – but not all beer drinkers feel like this. The other potential issue, which affects all drinkers of the brand, is the likelihood that the brewers and the beer they make will now be compromised, that brewers who were previously free to buy whatever ingredients and use whatever processes they wanted in order to make great beer would now have their wings clipped by accountants looking to cut costs, and marketing departments seeking to broaden the appeal of the beer as widely as possible.

Again, it's quite reasonable to make this assumption, and it's easy to point to beers where this has happened. But it's not *definite* that it will happen, and it's also easy to point to examples where it hasn't. Often, examples of both can exist even within the same corporation.

It is my opinion that Anheuser-Busch InBev has committed more sins against beer than any other large brewing corporation. I believe that the key decision-makers at the top of this organisation don't particularly care for beer at all, and are motivated solely by perpetual business growth and some kind of corporate ego-driven lust for market dominance. They have destroyed the integrity of beer after beer. One former brewer told me of the time his department had to sit through a presentation from a

(Penguin, London, 2014) p. 416

marketing manager who held up a can of one of their beers and said, "What's inside this can is irrelevant. It doesn't matter. Pointing to the logo, he said, "The only thing that matters is what's on the outside of the can." The brewer left soon after.

But AB InBev also employs Mike Siegel.

Mike runs research and development at the Goose Island brewery in Chicago. As we know, Goose Island hasn't been a "proper" craft brewery since it was acquired by AB InBev in 2011. But when you spend time with Mike, you have to keep pinching yourself to remember that. Twice, I've been lucky enough to spend the day with him in Chicago, hanging out at the brewery and going to see some of the new, independent craft brewers in Chicago that Mike thinks are worth a look. Many of the founders of these breweries are former Goose Island brewers themselves, some leaving because craft for them means not working for a corporation like AB InBev. Every now and then, they'll call Mike over an issue with quality control, infection or product inconsistencies, and he's always happy to drop by and help them work out what's wrong.

Back at the brewery, Mike's passion is the barrel-ageing programme: the vast warehouse of bourbon barrels that help create Bourbon County, arguably the world's most revered barrel-aged stout; and also the wine barrels that create spritzy Belgian-inspired beers such as Sophie and Gillian.

The last time I saw Mike was when he was over in the UK launching Obadiah Poundage, a collaboration with Wimbledon Brewing and beer historian Ron Pattinson, which sought to accurately recreate the flavour and character of a vatted mid-19th-century porter. It was a project two years in the making, with the beer brewed and aged in Chicago.

In the eyes of the small, independent beer industry, Goose Island may not be a craft brewery. But Mike Siegel brews great craft beer and behaves every bit like we would expect a great craft brewer to behave. In this, he is in a far from unique situation.

If we look at craft beer in its rightful place within the broader context of craft, we get a different slant on the importance of independence. It's far less about independence of ownership and far more about the independence of thought and action the brewer enjoys. Their autonomy over their labour and the results of it are what truly count in whether they are a craft brewer or not and whether the beer they make is a craft beer. Small, independent craft breweries are far more likely to offer this freedom and autonomy to their brewers, but not exclusively so. If we like, we can question the motives of corporations such as AB InBev in allowing their "craft" brewers a degree of autonomy they don't allow in their mainstream operations, but if those brewers are given control and direction over their labour, behave like we expect craft brewers to behave and subsequently create beers that are indistinguishable from independently owned craft beers, then they are craft brewers, brewing craft beer.

4. Motivation

A big part of the confusion over what craft beer is or isn't rests on the significant likelihood that brewers, hardcore craft beer fans and the broader drinking public risk talking at cross-purposes when discussing craft beer.

For some, it's about the independence/identity/ownership of the brewery. For others, it's about a vaguer, less defined set of values centred around supporting small, local business, being – and being seen as – anti-establishment or counter-cultural. And for many, craft beer is simply about the character of the beer. There's a strong Venn overlap between all these motivations, but they remain quite different.

When we have discussions about the nature and meaning of craft beer, many of us speak from an emotional, passionate point of view. And maybe it's because we don't want our honest emotions to show, or maybe it's because we want to appear more authoritative, or maybe it's simply because we aren't in touch with our emotions and aware of how they drive our behaviour, but we often attempt to cover or justify our emotional attachment to craft beer with rational analysis. Instead of trying to rationalise why so many of us are so drawn to an idea of "craft beer" that we cannot collectively pin down and agree on in rational, definitional terms, maybe we should instead explore, even celebrate, why craft beer provokes such a strong emotional response.

Craft beer and mainstream beer may be wildly different as beers, but they're very similar in a more meaningful aspect: both are cultural products at least as much as they are alcoholic liquid products. Whether you buy a slab of Bud or a bottle of Pliny the Younger, you have an emotional investment in that purchase. Other beers offering similar functional benefits are available. This is the one that feels right for you.

If you've read this far, I'm guessing you're more of a Pliny than a Bud person. What can I say? I know how people work. You probably tell yourself that you have consciously rejected mainstream brands built on multi-million-dollar marketing budgets. You're too clever to be sucked in by that. But if you'd still consider queuing overnight to get that coveted beer on the day of its release, you're obeying the same impulse as the guy who sips his suds while watching the Super Bowl ad.

Don't try to deny it, and at the same time, don't beat yourself up about it. This behaviour simply obeys the rules of craft in its wider context. Your functional needs – be they refreshment, intoxication, sitting down on a comfy chair or having a glass that holds the liquid you pour into it without leaking, breaking or falling over – can be met by a wider choice of cheap, mass-produced products than you will ever need. When you buy craft, the premium you're paying is buying something else.

Peter Korn describes craft purchases as being "economically marginal": where it was once necessary to buy hand-crafted products because there were no other alternatives available, in the cold logic of economics, there is now no functional need for crafted products at all given the availability of cheaper, reliable alternatives. The value in craft products is the value we decide to give them. So if we're being honest with ourselves, what are the emotional, or spiritual, sources of value in craft beer?

Craft beer wouldn't be what it is if it didn't offer several, powerful emotional rewards. A big one is that it satisfies a yearning for connection and continuity. We've talked at length about nostalgia, and about the alienation that the information age can make us feel. It's no coincidence that millennials – the first "digitally native" generation – responded more strongly to craft, in beer and elsewhere, than anyone else. Combine this with the decade of uncertainty and hardship that followed the global financial crash, and the attraction of craft is obvious. The scarier the present feels, and the more disengaged with it we feel, the more we look for something to re-engage with, something to ground us.

We might not be able to articulate this feeling of alienation, but if we're into craft, we're drawn to the idea of, and feel an implicit satisfaction from, getting things back onto a human scale. We want to get closer to the makers of the things we love, so we seek out brewers local to us, we attend "Meet the Brewer" events, and we start to choose taprooms over pubs.

Back when I worked in Big Beer marketing, we talked a lot

189

about provenance: In the 1980s and '90s, the country a beer came from was more important than how it tasted. Shit, why do you think anyone drinks Corona? (Or rather, used to drink Corona?) People do everything they can to disguise its rancid taste, but drink it because it transports them to a golden beach. Why do people get upset when they find out that Stella Artois is brewed in South Wales, or Doom Bar is brewed in Burton-on-Trent? In my advertising days, we always used to say that British provenance was not "aspirational" enough. Any big brand had to come from somewhere cool. For craft beer lovers, the idea of provenance still holds strong, even though aspirational provenance is no longer a foreign beach, but a local industrial estate.

This has happened because we now prize "authenticity" above all else. In an era of fake news, spin and manufactured celebrity, we seek out products and experiences that are – or feel like they are – unmediated and honest.

Like nostalgia, authenticity is a problematic concept. In his book *The Authenticity Hoax: why the "real" things we seek don't make us happy* (2010), Andrew Potter argues that authenticity has simply replaced "cool" as a universal aspiration and indication of social status.[120] When anyone can Google the hottest new music act and instantly stream their work on Spotify, the status that used to come with finding out about them and being able to claim you were into them before anyone else has evaporated. Instead, what you can do is shop at a farmer's market instead of a supermarket, correct someone's pronunciation of a Spanish food dish because you ate it all the time when you were in Barcelona, or laugh knowingly at the local "authentic Italian restaurant" that features spaghetti Bolognaise in its menu.

---

[120]Potter, Andrew, *The Authenticity Hoax: Why The "Real" Things We Seek Don't Make Us Happy* (Harper Perennial, Canada, 2010).

In the cynical, self-reflexive world of marketing, the Authenticity Dollar is big business. I once Googled "authentic travel experience" as an experiment and the compounding chain reaction of contradictions and paradoxes that resulted almost blew my brain out of my eye sockets. The all-out assault on the meaning of the word "authentic" makes our problems around "craft" look as easy as shooting fish off a log.

But the reason the A-word receives so much abuse is that it answers a genuine need: the need to engage with life and the world around us in meaningful way.

Craft brewers are heroes to the millions of people who crave greater authenticity and a more meaningful connection with the world. They're the ones who ditched the rat race and took that bold leap into the unknown, following their hearts rather than their wallets. Those of us still chained to the screen and the spreadsheet, lacking the courage or the ability to make that jump, live through them vicariously.

Richard Sennett's central argument in *The Craftsman* is that craft gives us an insight into human relations in their broadest sense. The lessons of craft are not just about how to make things well for their own sake, but amount to a "manual for living":

> Both the difficulties and the possibilities of making things well apply to making human relationships… Material challenges like working with resistance or managing ambiguity are instructive in understanding the resistances people harbour to one another or the uncertain boundaries between people. I've stressed the positive, open role routine and practicing play in the work of crafting physical things; so too do people need to practice their relations with one another, learn the skills of anticipation and revision in order to improve these relations.[121]

---

[121]Sennett, 2017, p.289.

Craft is the opposite of "computer says no". It isn't just about the things we make; it's about the kind of people we are. And from this, we get to an unspoken assumption that we may be reluctant to admit even to ourselves: we believe that makers and buyers of craft products are morally superior to other people.

This goes all the way back to the Arts & Crafts movement: Ruskin and Morris believed that the means of production affected the moral development of the worker, and that the objects produced affected the moral development of the consumer. How often have you heard phrases along the lines of "craft beer people are good people" or "good people drink good beer?" Why do we automatically expect craft brewers to have a progressive agenda?

From the craft drinker's perspective then, it's important that a craft brewer "means it," that their intentions are good, that they are buying into craft for the same emotional reasons we are. Sennett argues that "motivation is a more important issue than talent in consummating craftsmanship," which is not to say that talent is not important – I've argued as to why it is – but the intentions behind the beer are at least as important.

The issue here is that it's never a good look to argue that you are morally right or superior – these things absolutely have to be demonstrated rather than simply claimed. So if we're trying to argue about what is or isn't truly craft, it's easier to try to rationalise this emotional aspect by trying to fix it in more tangible terms. This is why "small" and "independent" feel so right when we're trying to define a craft brewery. But they only *feel* right because of the values they embody. Once again, it's far more likely that a small, independent brewery will have the right motivations and be consistent with the ideals and morality of craft, and far less likely that a large corporate will. But again, it's a Venn diagram overlap rather than a 100 per cent correlation.

My definition of a boombastic beer style

Having travelled in a very different direction, we've arrived in territory that is somewhat similar to Dan Shelton's widely ignored definition of craft beer discussed at the end of Part One. It would be a simple task to fashion my four pillars of skill/creativity, quality, autonomy and motivation into a tight summary that would make much more sense and be far truer to what craft beer really is than the "official" definitions of the past.

The reason I haven't done so is that, as is the case with Shelton's definition, you could never measure it to decide whether any given brewery is "craft" or not. And for the people who are keenest to have a tight definition of craft beer, measurement is the whole point of having such a definition. Surely a non-measurable definition is utterly useless?

I can understand why someone would believe that. But if they do, they've missed the whole point of craft.

The inability to measure, to calibrate, to monitor, to pin down and replicate, is precisely what sets craft apart from the mainstream in any context, and beer is no exception.

Unlike most brewers today, Sierra Nevada only uses whole leaf hops, not pellets. That's because, back in the 1980s, the brewery split a batch of its Celebration Ale and hopped half with pellets and half with flowers. Every measurable variable was identical. But when the team tasted the two beers side by side, without knowing which was which, everyone preferred the whole flower brew.

Similarly, Crisp Maltings in Norfolk produces most of its brewing malt using modern drum technology. They have no choice: a traditional floor maltings used to do 10,000 tonnes of malt a year. Crisp now does that in a week. There aren't enough floors around to meet the demand from breweries, not to mention that floor malting is backbreaking work. And yet, as craft brewers engage with where their malt comes from, they're increasingly asking Crisp specifically for floor malted barley. In its physicality, by-hand nature, small batches and long tradition, floor malting is undeniably a craft process. It's a great story and it gives both the brewer and drinker a nice feeling, but it's also more than that. When I visited Crisp while writing *Miracle Brew,* Dr Dave Griggs, the Group Technical Director, told me, "When you do the technical analysis between floor malting and drum malting, they're absolutely identical. But if you give it to people in blind taste tests, they can pick up a real difference". There has to be a reason for this. But whatever it is, the world's leading experts don't know what it is and can't measure it. Dave Griggs can only make highly educated guesses. "Three days in the kiln as opposed to 24 hours might have something to do with it, as might the difference in air movement – volatile aroma compounds won't get blown off if it's gentle. Maybe with a bigger drum, we drive off those volatiles."

Craft skills cannot be fully broken down into steps and processes by scientific management, and that's why industrial production loses something. Break the process of making a product down into as many steps and components as possible. Measure them. Record them. Replicate them as a scientific process. The piece that's still missing is craft – the skills and talents that Sturt's wheelwrights were unable to explain to him. It's therefore completely understandable and entirely appropriate that an accurate, fair and comprehensible definition of "craft beer" should be similarly unmeasurable.

Conclusion: so why bother?

Only in a field as counter-intuitive and complicated as craft beer could spectacular success bring such intractable problems with it. I imagine there must be longstanding craft brewers wishing bitterly that craft beer was still an underground scene that was ignored by the mainstream. It was all so simple back then: we knew who the enemy was, and we could talk to each other as loudly as we wanted about how great the beer was, safe in the knowledge that no one would hear us, and even if they did, they would pay no attention.

Damn those jerks for listening.

Across Europe, a majority of all beer drinkers in Poland (64%), France (63%) and Italy (61%) claim to be interested in trying different types of craft beer such as IPAs, and around half of all beer drinkers in Italy (52%), France (51%), Germany (46%) and the UK (45%) agree that craft beer "is worth the extra money".[122] In 2018, the global craft beer market was valued at US$37.54bn and was forecast to reach over $92bn by 2025.[123] It doesn't matter whether these people are drinking "true craft beer" or not, or whether they can define craft beer or not: the whole notion of craft beer has outgrown the tight circle that cares about these issues. Craft beer doesn't belong to us any more.

It's an entirely understandable reaction to this that the hardcore craft beer scene – the small, independent brewers who pioneer the taste and values of craft and the people who drink the beers and share those values – might throw their hands up and abandon the term, especially when we could never agree on what it meant in the first place.

"Craft beer" was never the right term to define and protect small, independent brewers. "Independent" or "indie" will do that necessary and important job far better. So do we still need the term "craft beer"?

___

[122]https://www.mintel.com/press-centre/food-and-drink/europe-now-dominates-craft-beer-innovation
[123]https://www.globenewswire.com/news-release/2019/01/25/1705363/0/en/Global-Craft-Beer-Market-Will-Reach-USD-92-230-Million-By-2025-Zion-Market-Research.html

Oh, reason not the need. Haven't you been paying attention? Craft is not about *needs*, it's about something bigger and better. Also, no one – not an industry body, a brewer nor a craft beer geek – gets to say that craft beer is dead or redundant or meaningless. It's out there now, being used by millions of people, living as words live.

It's another entirely understandable reaction to suggest that "true craft" should simply choose a different term, like "artisanal" or "small-batch" to maintain its differentiation from mass craft. At this stage, I think we can agree that any alternative term would suffer the same fate "craft beer" has, without being as powerful or evocative to begin with.

I still think – for all the reasons I've explained – that the term "craft beer" is worth fighting for, worth attempting to keep a stake in, and worth discussing. The definition of craft beer has always focused on protecting the interests of a group of brewers. Freed from that task, it can now be used by drinkers to hold brewers accountable, large and small alike, and to inspire and engage people with the true value of what those brewers do, and how they do it.

I began this final part of the book by talking about words as building blocks, and about how different words that have very similar meanings can work in quite different ways when we shove them into a sentence. I also talked about how words can change their meanings over time. Put these two very simple concepts together and you start to get to the deep philosophy behind language – and meaning – pretty quickly. Letters and words are just shapes on a page or stone tablet. Like that tree in the forest that attracts so much concern over whether or not it makes a sound when it falls over, letters and words stand there like anatomically awkward contestants in a talent show, waiting for us to pick them.

Ferdinand de Saussure introduced the notion of semiotics to the study of language. He argued that words only have meaning in relation to each other, in the way that the role and power of chess pieces are not related to the shapes of the pieces, but by the relationships between the pieces, and the meanings we confer on those relationships. Semiotics works on the logic that a meaningful sign has two components: the signifier – a physical word, object, sound or symbol – and the signified – a mental concept or meaning. While signifiers might change little over time, the signified concept can change between people and context. A red rose means romance. But the colour red in a cross might signify medical help. Draw that red cross differently, and it's a flag that could mean English patriotism, far right racism or the Christian persecution of Muslims, depending on where it is, and who you are.

Peter Korn comes close to this when he returns to the topic of defining craft from his perspective of transforming wood into furniture, which puts our current debate about the term "craft beer" into a much broader perspective:

> When it comes to definition, craft is a moving target. Like its cousins art and design, craft is a cultural construct that evolves in response to changing mindsets and conditions of society... The best way to understand craft, I believe, is to think of it as a conversation flowing through time. Or, more precisely, as a recent eddy in a broad conversation about object making that began at least 2.5 million years ago.[124]

This book has argued that "craft beer" is undefinable and misunderstood. I also don't deny that the term is horrendously abused and taken advantage of. Its meaning has shifted over time and continues to do so, but I think that demonstrates why we do need it rather than why we should retire it. It signifies a heady brew of ideas and feelings that, if we explore them fully, reveal so much more to us about ourselves, our world and how we experience it, than any other term could do, and certainly more than "independent" ever will. For all its weaknesses – not least

---

[124]Korn, 2017, p.31.

the certainty that it will always lack a measurable definition – my argument is that the term "craft beer" remains absolutely essential.

If you find it difficult to continue to use and support a phrase that can't be pinned down, the post-structuralists who critiqued Saussure's work have come up with a useful solution which I offer here as a compromise – because compromise, remember, can sometimes be a positive move.

For some twentieth century thinkers, this whole "signifier and signified" thing, with the allowance that signifiers are unstable and can change meaning over time, was just a little too neat. The paradox that they had to use words in order to meaningfully convey their scepticism of the idea that words successfully conveyed meaning was not lost on them. German Philosopher Martin Heidegger came up with a solution. He started using words, and crossing them out but leaving them in place and legible, without offering an alternative word instead, a practice he termed *sous rature*, or "under erasure". "Since the word is inaccurate, it is crossed out," he explained. "Since it is necessary, it remains legible."

Sometimes, the words we have may not be perfect, but they're the best we've got at doing the job. Which is why, for me, I will always continue to drink, write about, celebrate and argue over ~~craft beer~~.

198

Postscript:
You think *we've* got problems?

I am honoured to be able to call Richard Boon a good friend. It's weird knowing him. You talk to some people and explain who he is and they nod and smile politely, their eyes telegraphing something along the lines of "Are you seriously expecting me to have ever heard of this person?" And then, other times, I might mention his name in passing and people will freeze, look me in the eye and say, "What? THE Richard Boon? Seriously? How on earth do you know him?" and proceed to freak out, pleading for an introduction.

Richard went to school with Howard Devoto, a founder member of Buzzcocks. When the band came together, Richard became their manager because, in his telling, he was the only one who lived in a house with a telephone. Rather than sign to one of the major labels in London, Richard founded his own record label in Manchester, New Hormones, which released Buzzcocks's legendary "Spiral Scratch" EP, commonly regarded as the first "independent" single release into a market that was choked by the collective dominance of a handful of corporate record labels.

Richard then proceeded to be a mover and shaker behind the scenes, quietly guiding the development of the Manchester punk scene as it evolved first into New Wave, and then into Indie. Eventually he moved to London and worked for Rough Trade records. Along the way, he gave help, guidance and support to bands including The Fall, Joy Division, New Order and The Smiths. Sonic Youth used to sleep on his floor. Even Morrissey is nice about Richard in his dreadful autobiography. And for real eighties indie heads out there, he persuaded Rough Trade to release Camper Van Beethoven's "Take the Skinheads Bowling".

When Rough Trade collapsed, Richard left the music business, and after staying at home to raise his children, eventually became a librarian in Stoke Newington, and ultimately a key figure in the Stoke Newington Literary Festival, founded and run by my wife Liz Vater in 2010. I first met him when we launched *Man Walks into a Pub* (2003) at the Stoke Newington Bookshop. He likes his beer, and like any good punk, he likes his structural theory. When I explained my ambition for the book, which was to write about beer from a socio-cultural point of view rather than a straightforward food and drink appreciation angle, he became intense and slightly mocking at the same time, and kept asking himself, "What would Dewey do?" We've been friends ever since.

In 2016 – the "official" anniversary of the birth of the punk rock movement – Richard was invited onto a discussion panel at the Museum of London featuring various other luminaries from the punk era, to kick off a citywide celebration of punk's 40th birthday. The intention had been to discuss a range of issues. Instead the panel were quickly drawn into an argument – with heated contributions from members of the audience, some of whom obviously thought they should have been on the panel instead – about the definition of punk, and if there was one. Remembering the origin of the word "revolution", the discussion went around in circles until it was time to wrap up.

It's fair to characterise punk as a revolution – a short, sharp shock that caused irreparable harm to the system that preceded it, and ensured that whatever status quo came after it would – well – feature far less Status Quo. But punk was nasty, brutish and short, a quick shiv to the kidneys of popular culture that came and went within the space of three years, leaving behind only a London postcard cliché of leather-clad Mohicans in Piccadilly Circus, and an attitude that resonates with every single generation that's picked up a guitar since. Punk is a debased, exploited and fatuous cliché, and it's also an energy that keeps music alive four decades on. How can you reconcile its contradictory meanings?

You can't. Sorry.

Punk is far too influential to be summed up in the neat terms of a precise definition. Even the people who created it can't do that. Though I'm sure they wish they could.

As I said, Richard Boon's career extended beyond punk and he became a key figure in the "indie" scene that moved music on through the 1980s. And this is how I first met Richard King. I'm sorry they're both called Richard, but it's really not my fault. I first met Richard (King) when he was trying to get as much time as possible to interview Richard (Boon) for a book he was writing. That book was eventually released as *How Soon Is Now: The madmen and mavericks who made independent music 1975-2005* (which also featured extensive interviews with my other friend Richard Thomas, who used to promote New Order, but I'm sensing this is getting complicated now).

Richards Boon, King and Thomas all turned out to be beer lovers, which suggests a correlation between beer and people called Richard, or between beer and people who are guiding lights in modern pop and rock music, and thereby, between beer and music itself.

I suspect it's the latter.

When *How Soon is Now* was published in 2012, we booked Richard (King) for our third Stoke Newington Literary Festival. It being Stoke Newington, where '80s indie kids of every strata from the former lead singer of The Steaming Trousers (me) all the way up to the lead singer and guitarist of Sonic Youth (Thurston Moore) eventually seem to congregate, Richard (King) had a great gig. Afterwards, in a

201

bar that had been stocked with beers from our newly emerging local craft breweries, he asked me what defined a true craft brewery.

I started talking about size, independence of ownership, and use of traditional ingredients versus the need for innovation. Richard (King) was definitely interested, which I could tell from the questions he was asking. But a smile started to appear like a structural crack on his face. The crack spread, and quickly, his entire body collapsed.

Had he been winding me up?

"No, no, not at all," he said, "I was genuinely curious, because I think craft beer is a really interesting idea. But every single thing you've just said repeats, word for word, the arguments that were happening on music blogs about the meaning of 'indie music' ten years ago. Best of luck."

Craft beer is an enigma, something that inspires both a people's movement and a multi-billion-dollar global industry, while at the same time creating heated argument within its most passionate adherents about what it actually is and whether it even exists or not. We may think this enigma is unique. But as I've found consistently throughout my career as a beer writer, music got there first.

Twice.

Punk IPA? "Indie beer"? Be careful what you wish for.

Further reading

This isn't a full bibliography (the notes are pretty exhaustive if you're looking for that) but these are the key texts I've relied on, and the best places I know to dig further into the themes covered in this book.

Acitelli, Tom, *The Audacity of Hops: The History of America's Craft Beer Revolution,* Chicago Review Press, Chicago, 2013.

Boak, Jessica, and Bailey, Ray, *Beer Britannia: The Strange Rebirth of British Beer,* Aurum, London, 2014.

Boym, Svetlana, *The Future of Nostalgia,* Basic Books, New York, 2002.

Brown, Pete, *The Apple Orchard: The Story of Our Most English Fruit*, Penguin, London, 2016.

Brown, Pete, *Miracle Brew: Adventures in the Nature of Beer*, Unbound, London, 2017.

Crawford, Matthew, *Shop Class as Soulcraft: An Inquiry into the Value of Work*, Penguin, New York, 2009. Published in the UK as *The Case for Working With Your Hands, or Why Office Work is Bad For Us and Fixing Things Feels Good*, Penguin, London, 2009.

Frayling, Christopher, *On Craftsmanship: Towards a New Bauhaus*, Oberon, London, 2017.

Hindy, Steve, *The Craft Beer Revolution: How a Band of Microbrewers Is Transforming the World's Favorite Drink*, St Martin's Press, New York, 2014.

Korn, Peter, *Why We Make Things and Why it Matters,* Vintage, London, 2017.

Langlands, Alexander, *Cræft: How Traditional Crafts Are About More Than Just Making,* Faber & Faber, London, 2017.

Noel, Josh, *Barrel Aged Stout and Selling Out: Goose Island, Anheuser-Busch, and How Craft Beer Became Big Business*, Chicago Review Press, Chicago, 2018.

Rail, Evan, *The Meanings of Craft Beer*, Kindle, 2016.

Sennett, Richard, *The Craftsman,* Penguin, London, 2009.

Sturt, George, *The Wheelright's Shop*, Cambridge University Press, Cambridge, 1930.

Van Munching, Philip: *Beer Blast: The Inside Story of the Brewing Industry's Bizarre Battles for Your Money*, Crown Business, New York, 1997.

Webb, Tim, *Good Beer Guide Belgium,* 6th edition, CAMRA, St Albans, 2009.

Wilson, Colin, *The Outsider*, Victor Gollancz, London, 1956.

About the author

Pete Brown is a British writer, journalist, broadcaster and consultant specialising in food and drink, especially the fun parts like beer, pubs, cider, bacon rolls, and fish and chips.

Across ten books, his broad, fresh approach takes in social history, cultural commentary, travel writing, personal discovery and natural history, and his words are always delivered with the warmth and wit you'd expect from a great night down the pub.

He writes for newspapers and magazines around the world and is a regular contributor to BBC Radio 4's Food Programme. He was named British Beer Writer of the Year in 2009, 2012 and 2016, has won three Fortnum & Mason Food and Drink Awards, and has been shortlisted twice for the Andre Simon Awards. Pete is Chair of the British Guild of Beer Writers.

He lives in London with his wife Liz, and dog Mildred.

http://petebrown.net
Social: @petebrownbeer

Other books by Pete Brown

Man Walks into a Pub:
A Sociable History of Beer

Three Sheets to the Wind:
One Man's Quest For The Meaning of Beer

Hops & Glory:
One Man's Search For The Beer That Built The British Empire

Shakespeare's Local:
Six Centuries of Everyday Life Seen Through One Extraordinary Pub

World's Best Cider:
Taste, Tradition and Terroir, from Somerset to Seattle

The Pub:
A Cultural Institution – from Country Inns to Craft Beer Bars and Corner Locals

The Apple Orchard:
The Story of Our Most English Fruit

Miracle Brew:
Adventures in the Nature of Beer

Pie Fidelity:
In Defence of British Food

Additional thanks

I'd expressly like to thank the following people for signing up to support this book via Patreon:

James Beech
Matthew Black
Justin Cooper
James Grinter
Stephen Reynolds
Peter Hudák
Roger Kille
Will Laithwaite
Steve Lamond
Eddie Marshall
Dipak Nayar
Andy Slee
Mark Smith-Magee
Unity Brewing

Look out for more exclusive content, benefits and offers at https://www.patreon.com/petebrownbeer

Printed in Great Britain
by Amazon

64542981R00123